Learning from Hollywood

Hans Dieter Schaal

Learning from Hollywood

Architecture and Film
Architektur und Film

Edition Axel Menges

Published in cooperation with the Stiftung Deutsche Kinemathek, Berlin.
Veröffentlicht in Zusammenarbeit mit der Stiftung Deutsche Kinemathek, Berlin.

ISBN 978-3-936681-34-5

Third edition
Dritte Auflage

Reproductions/Reproduktionen: Bild und Text GmbH Baun, Fellbach
Printing and binding/Druck und Bindearbeiten: Graspo CZ, a.s., Zlín, Tschechische Republik/Czech Republic

Translation into English/Übersetzung ins Englische: Michael Robinson

Editing/Lektorat: Dorothea Duwe
Layout: Helga Danz

Wolfgang Jacobsen

Time-travel in time-space

The Tower of Babel in Fritz Lang's *Metropolis* is yesterday and tomorrow. It is a piece of urban fantasy. The hillside bungalow in Alfred Hitchcock's *North by Northwest*, chained like Prometheus, is present becoming future. Film architecture has sign character. Whether it is reality, illusion or fantasy – film architecture plays a quite particular role. Film is a sign language.

The first to come to mind are *Metropolis* and American urban Utopias in the films of the eighties and nineties, *Blade Runner*, of course. Attention is directed entirely at the mountains of skyscrapers, monstrous pyramidic excrescences of a city growing rampantly into the sky. Glorification and excessive elevation, visions that are often apocalyptic, or invocations of new worlds. Next to these are the Piranesi-inspired Carceri, apparently out of sight and yet in the centre, caves from a counter-world that is striving into the dark and often hides secrets of light. All this can sink into a great Atlantis flood – as in Fritz Lang, and almost as a metaphor for the existence of film architecture – in order to resurface years later as a deciphered new cipher in Kevin Costner's *Waterworld*. Enigma.

And we also catch sight of visions of Murnau's *Sunrise* and Coppola's *One from the Heart*, alternating between architectural designs of city and nature, in which the city appears as an amusement park and the countryside as a symbol of capricious life; nature proves to be as artificial as the glittering façades of the big small towns, which are craft and computer imagination – in fact sign language, condensed into pictorial worlds, eclectic or independently emotional and creative.

Is film architecture real? Is architecture real? The hotel in Visconti's *Death in Venice* or the sanatorium high up in Davos in Geissendörfer's *The Magic Mountain*? Erich von Stroheim's crazy Monte Carlo in *Foolish Wives* or the grandiose but false Carlton Hotel in the Chanel videoclip? Where are *Lindenstraße* and *Berlin-Alexanderplatz*? They are also connected by the wilful inventive intoxication of a man like Rotwang or Dr. Emmett Brown: *Back to the Future*.

A look inside, just a detail: nature has been brought »home« in the urban space, preserved in props. It is unmoved, a silent guest: framed landscape images, postcards stuck behind mirrors; and of course the architecture of furnishings, that too is a landscape. In the city nature is static. It can be turned around, put away, substituted. Often such props mark the intersection of dream and reality.

For a long time the look has bordered on the immeasurable, for a long time our understanding of nature has been occupied by the compulsive notions of a dream city. Michelangelo Antonioni's *The Red Desert* transforms the landscape into an artful experiment with reality, at the same time a distorted image and a filmic puzzle. Film architecture is a mixtum compositum or Cinéplastique, not just an architecture of motion but architecture in motion. Futuristic worlds and mythic-archaic spaces are intended to become real and earthly, but also to be Science Fiction: time promises. What do Pasolini's *Oedipus Rex* and Stanley Kubrick's *2001* have in common, or Ridley Scott's *Blade Runner* and William Wyler's *Ben Hur*? They are projections of our wishes, that (are allowed) take to shape in ever new and varied worlds from the architects' workshops. And however near, however tangible film architecture ultimately may be, it also remains terrain vague, fleeting, a mere impression, rapid eye movement.

It is very tempting to keep on being drawn into a métier where the built Utopias of reality are close on the one hand, but also remain a mere reflection, fantasy and fiction. Time-travel in time-space. Hovering between the garden landscapes in Ludwig Berger's *Ein Glas Wasser*, Alain Resnais' *L'année dernière à Marienbad* and Peter Greenaway's *The Draughtsman's Contract*; strolling through the claustrophobic interiors of an Expressionist film and the American-style living-kitchen, with Doris Day at work at the cooker; escaping from the childlike and naïve fantasy universe of a director like Georges Méliès into the hermetic spaces of the James Bond worlds, in which floors, ceilings and walls can open and make the architecture disappear along with the people; and then escaping into the computer-animated data architecture of an architect like Zbig Rybczynski. Film is a laboratory of modernism. Film architecture is a laboratory of film modernism.

On the trail of a historical cross-section of pictorial worlds – here looking in from the outside, not with the eye of a film architect but that of a cineastic architect, testing his own visions against the film, discovering ciphers, decoding signs, like an architectural Marco Polo on a journey of exploration in the pictorial space between reality and fiction. Hans Dieter

Schaal writes: »It is no longer enough today to study architectural history, one also has to know film history, with its images, spaces and architectures.« A story of the power of images is also being told.

Films show particles of reality, even when they seem to be unambiguously dreamed. Moments of time are preserved in them. Hans Dieter Schaal puts the case for opening up the workshops and inventors' rooms. For perceiving something of what others get up to with one's own métier and vocabulary. For reflecting on imaginative capacities, for examining montage structures. An architectural sketch is to be read like a screenplay and conversely the film script like a building plan. If the reader is prepared to enter into this mind game it leads to digressions that run right through the history of architecture and film. There are parallel lines that meet at infinity and there are intersections where it is no longer possible to distinguish whether film is driving architecture or architecture film. Readers should also see this book as an architectural sketch and a film script ...

Wolfgang Jacobsen

Zeitreisen in Zeiträumen

Der Turm zu Babel in Fritz Langs *Metropolis* ist Gestern und Morgen. Er ist ein Stück Stadtphantasie. Der an den Berghang gebaute Bungalow in Alfred Hitchcocks *North by Northwest*, wie Prometheus an die Kette gelegt, ist Gegenwart, die Zukunft wird, Filmarchitektur hat Zeichencharakter. Ob Realität, Illusion oder Phantasie – die Architektur im Film spielt eine eigene Rolle. Der Film ist eine Zeichensprache.

In den Blick kommen zunächst *Metropolis* und die amerikanischen Stadtutopien in Filmen der achtziger und neunziger Jahre, *Blade Runner* natürlich. Die ganze Aufmerksamkeit richtet sich auf die Wolkenkratzergebirge, die monströsen pyramidalen Auswüchse einer in den Himmel wuchernden Stadt, Glorifizierungen und Überhöhungen, Endzeitvisionen oftmals oder Beschwörungen neuer Welten. Und daneben finden sich die von Piranesi inspirierten Carceri, wie aus dem Blick geraten und doch im Zentrum, Höhlen einer Gegenwelt, die ins Dunkle strebt und oft lichte Geheimnisse birgt. Dies alles kann in einer großen Atlantisflut versinken – wie bei Fritz Lang und fast als eine Metapher für die Existenz der Filmarchitektur –, um Jahrzehnte später als dechiffrierte neue Chiffre in Kevin Costners *Waterworld* wieder aufzutauchen. Enigma.

Und in den Blick kommen auch die Visionen von Murnaus *Sunrise* und Coppolas *One from the Heart,* alternierend zwischen den architektonischen Entwürfen von Stadt und Natur, in denen die Stadt als Vergnügungspark erscheint und das Land als Sinnbild wetterwendischen Lebens, und die Natur sich so künstlich zeigt wie die glitzernden Fassaden der großen kleinen Städte, die Handwerk sind und Computerimagination – Zeichensprache eben, zu Bilderwelten verdichtet, eklektizistisch oder eigenständig emotional und kreativ.

Ist Filmarchitektur wirklich? Ist Architektur wirklich? Das Hotel in Viscontis *La morte a Venezia* oder das Sanatorium auf den Höhen von Davos in Geissendörfers *Der Zauberberg*? Das aberwitzige Monte Carlo des Erich von Stroheim in *Foolish Wives* oder das grandios-falsche Carlton-Hotel im Video-Clip für Chanel? Wo sind die *Lindenstraße* und *Berlin-Alexanderplatz*? Was sie auch miteinander verbindet, ist der eigensinnige Erfinderrausch eines Rotwang oder Dr. Emmett Brown: *Back to the Future*.

Ein Blick nach innen, nur ein Ausschnitt: Im städtischen Raum ist die Natur »heimgeholt«. Sie ist aufgehoben in Requisiten. Sie ist unentwegt ein stummer Gast: gerahmte Landschaftsbilder, hinter Spiegel gesteckte Postkarten; und natürlich die Architektur des Mobiliars, auch sie eine Landschaft. In der Stadt ist die Natur statisch. Man kann sie umdrehen, wegstellen, austauschen. Oft markieren diese Requisiten Schnittstellen zwischen Traum und Wirklichkeit.

Längst ufert der Blick ins Unermeßliche, längst ist das Verständnis von Natur mit den Zwangsvorstellungen einer Traumstadt besetzt. *Il deserto rosso von* Michelangelo Antonioni überführt die Landschaft in ein kunstvolles Wirklichkeitsexperiment, Zerrbild und filmisches Vexierspiel zugleich. Filmische Architektur ist ein Mixtum compositum oder Cinéplastique, eine Architektur nicht nur in der Bewegung, sondern eine Architektur in Bewegung. Futuristische Welten und mythisch archaische Räume sollen real, irdisch werden, aber eben auch Science fiction sein: Zeitversprechen. Was haben Pasolinis *Edipo re* und Stanley Kubricks *2001* gemeinsam, was Ridley Scotts *Blade Runner* und William Wylers *Ben Hur*? Sie sind Projektionen unserer Wünsche, die Gestalt annehmen (dürfen) in immer neuen, variierten Welten aus der Werkstatt der Architekten. Und so nah, so zum Greifen sichtbar Filmarchitektur letztlich auch sein mag, sie bleibt auch terrain vague, flüchtig, ein Eindruck nur, rapid eye movement.

Die Versuchung ist groß, sich immer wieder auf ein Metier einzulassen, wo die gebauten Utopien der Realität einerseits nahe sind, andererseits aber doch nur Spiegelung, Phantasie und Fiktion bleiben. Zeitreisen in Zeiträumen. Schweben zwischen den Gartenlandschaften in Ludwig Bergers *Ein Glas Wasser,* Alain Resnais' *L'année dernière à Marienbad* und Peter Greenaways *The Draughtsman's Contract*; flanieren zwischen den klaustrophoben Innenräumen eines expressionistischen Films und der Wohnküche American style, in der Doris Day am Herd hantiert, fliehen aus dem kindlich naiven Phantasie-Universum eines Georges Méliès in die hermetischen Räume der James-Bond-Welten, in denen sich Böden, Decken, Wände öffnen können und mit den Menschen auch die Architektur verschwinden lassen; und sich flüchten in die computeranimierte Datenarchitektur eines Zbig Rybczynski. Der Film ist ein Laboratorium der Moderne. Filmarchitektur ist ein Laboratorium der filmischen Moderne.

Den Bilderwelten nachspüren quer durch die Geschichte – hier mit dem Blick von außen, nicht dem eines Filmarchitekten, sondern eines cineastischen Architekten, der seine eigenen Visionen an Filmen prüft, Chiffren entdeckt, Zeichen entschlüsselt, wie ein Marco Polo der Architektur auf Entdeckungsreise im Bilderraum zwischen Realität und Fiktion. Hans Dieter Schaal schreibt: »Es genügt heute nicht mehr, Architekturgeschichte zu studieren, man muß auch die Filmgeschichte kennen, mit ihren Bildern, Räumen und Architekturen.« Erzählt wird also auch die Geschichte von der Kraft der Bilder.

Filme zeigen Partikel der Realität, selbst da, wo sie eindeutig geträumt scheinen. In ihnen aufgehoben sind Augenblicke der Zeit. Hans Dieter Schaal plädiert dafür, die Werkstätten und Erfinderstuben zu öffnen. Etwas wahrzunehmen von dem, was andere mit dem eigenen Metier und Vokabular anstellen. Einstellungsgrößen zu überdenken, Montagestrukturen zu prüfen. Die architektonische Skizze ist wie ein Drehbuch zu lesen und umgekehrt das filmische Skript wie ein Bauplan. Läßt man sich als Leser auf dieses Gedankenspiel ein, so ergeben sich Exkurse quer durch die Geschichte der Architektur und des Films. Es verlaufen Parallelen, die sich im Unendlichen treffen, und es finden sich Schnittpunkte, wo nicht mehr unterscheidbar ist, ob die Architektur den Film oder der Film die Architektur antreibt. Auch dieses Buch sollten die Leser als Architekturskizze und als Filmskript verstehen ...

To the subject

The concrete reason for more intensive investigation of the subject »Film and Architecture« was provided by preparing and designing architecture for the exhibition *Kino – Movie – Cinéma*, which took place in the Martin-Gropius-Bau (Berlin) in 1995, under the auspices of the Stiftung Deutsche Kinemathek. It was the medium's hundredth anniversary, and the exhibition used this as a reason for presenting some aspects of its ideas, history and development. The phenomenon that film cannot actually be exhibited was also addressed in some areas. This produced balancing acts between material and immaterial, reality and fiction, light and dark.

I was given the opportunity to travel to Hollywood, to talk to people who worked there on the spot and to visit figures like Josef von Sternberg's widow.

There are countless books on film as a medium, about stars, directors, cameramen and also about film architects. This book intends to examine the origins, function and effects of film's architectures and spaces and compare them with the real architectures and spaces of today's cities. Perhaps this could stimulate some interplay. Of course this look at the two worlds is not comprehensive, and the subjective preferences of an architect and film lover are unmistakable.

First a look at the place in which film architecture is created: the film studios. Film studios have their own atmosphere, they are places on the fringes of reality. Here physical things become metaphysical. Anything that is really built is usually only present in part, and made of impermanent materials. The walls have a face side and a second side with braces and rough board screens, which unmask them as lies and backdrops. This is a splendid place to reflect about the concepts of »truth« and »lies« in architecture.

My first real confrontation with the world of the film studio was in 1976, when I was able to look at the architecture and constructions for Federico Fellini's film *Casanova* while spending time in a Rome studio. Shooting had just ended but the palace rooms, corners of squares and house façades they represented were still standing. The surrealistic quality of the giant figures set up in the open air was so impressive that it will never leave the spaces of my fantasy and memory. A pall of the melancholy of something no longer used hung over everything. It was reminiscent of Bomarzo and the ruins of the Forum Romanum. The pieces will certainly have rotted in the mean time or have ended up on a rubbish tip.

Things like this are now often preserved in many of the world's film studios, recreated as sights within the studio tour.

Of course the artificiality of studio architecture is not suitable for every film. Films are often shot in real landscapes and cities. When you are standing in such a »scene of crime« illuminated by film spotlights and gigantic mirrors you start to ponder again about what reality, truth and fiction really are in film. Light becomes a crucial factor. At night in particular it transforms every square in the town into a metaphysical place. Anything illuminated becomes significant architecture. This place had previously not been noticed at all because it sank in a sea of urban banality, but now it can become a picture, pictorial architecture. Camera and film will later transform the place further, into the film image, the film detail, which again will become part of a pictorial sequence, of a whole.

We can learn from films and film images that the architecture of houses, streets and cities is not simply a problem of order, function and economic viability, but that psychology, atmosphere and images are also being constructed here.

Zum Thema

Konkreter Anlaß für die intensivere Beschäftigung mit dem Thema »Film und Architektur« waren die Vorbereitungs- und Entwurfsarbeiten zur Architektur der Ausstellung *Kino – Movie – Cinéma*, die 1995 – veranstaltet von der Stiftung Deutsche Kinemathek – im Martin-Gropius-Bau (Berlin) stattgefunden hat. Das Medium wurde hundert Jahre alt, und die Ausstellung nahm diesen Geburtstag zum Anlaß, einige Aspekte in ihrer Idee, ihrer Geschichte und ihrer Entfaltung darzustellen. Auch das Phänomen, daß sich Film eigentlich nicht ausstellen läßt, wurde in einigen Räumen reflektiert. So entstanden Gratwanderungen zwischen Immateriellem und Materiellem, zwischen Realität und Fiktion, zwischen Licht und Dunkel.

Für mich gab es die Möglichkeit, nach Hollywood zu reisen, vor Ort mit dortigen Akteuren zu sprechen und u. a. die Witwe von Josef von Sternberg zu besuchen.

Es gibt unzählige Bücher über das Medium Film, über die Stars, die Regisseure, die Kameramänner und auch über die Filmarchitekten. Dieses Buch will die Architekturen und Räume der Filme in ihrer Entstehung, ihrer Funktion und ihrer Wirkung untersuchen und sie mit den realen Architekturen und Räumen der Städte von heute vergleichen. Vielleicht können Wechselwirkungen angeregt werden. Natürlich ist der Blick auf beide Welten nicht umfassend, die subjektiven Vorlieben eines Architekten und leidenschaftlichen Filmfreundes sind nicht zu übersehen.

Zuerst ein Blick auf den Ort des Entstehens der Filmarchitekturen: die Filmstudios. Filmstudios haben ihre eigene Atmosphäre, sie sind Orte am Rande der Realität. Hier wird Physisches in Metaphysisches verwandelt. Tatsächlich Gebautes ist nur teilweise anwesend und meist aus vergänglichen Materialien hergestellt. Die Wände haben eine Gesichtsseite und eine zweite Seite mit Abstützungen und rohen Bretterwänden, die sie als Lüge und Kulisse entlarven. Man kann hier vortrefflich über die Begriffe »Wahrheit« und »Lüge« in der Architektur reflektieren.

Die erste reale Begegnung mit der Filmstudio-Welt hatte ich 1976, als ich während eines Studienaufenthalts in Rom die Architekturen und Aufbauten zu Federico Fellinis Film *Casanova* besichtigen konnte. Die Dreharbeiten waren gerade beendet, aber die angedeuteten Schloßräume, die Platzecken und Hausfassaden standen noch. Der Surrealismus der im Freien aufgebauten Riesenfiguren war so eindrucksvoll, daß er meine Phantasie- und Erinnerungsräume nie mehr verlassen wird. Über allem lag die Melancholie des Nicht-mehr-Gebrauchten. Man dachte an Bomarzo und die Ruinen des Forum Romanum. Inzwischen sind die Teile sicher längst zerfallen oder auf einer Müllkippe gelandet.

In vielen Filmstudios der Welt werden heute diese Dinge erhalten und zu Sehenswürdigkeiten innerhalb der Studiotours umfunktioniert.

Die Künstlichkeit der Atelierarchitektur ist nicht für jeden Film geeignet. Oft wird auch an realen Orten in Landschaften und Städten gedreht. Wenn man vor einem solchen von Filmscheinwerfern und riesigen Spiegeln ausgeleuchteten »Tatort« steht, kommt man wieder ins Grübeln, was Wirklichkeit, Wahrheit und Fiktion in der Architektur ist. Licht wird zum entscheidenden Faktor. Vor allem nachts verwandelt es jeden Platz der Stadt in einen metaphysischen Ort. Was beleuchtet ist, wird zur Bedeutungsarchitektur. Jetzt kann dieser Ort, der vorher so überhaupt nicht wahrgenommen wurde, weil er im Meer der Stadtbanalität untergegangen ist, zum Bild und zur Bildarchitektur werden. Die Kamera und die Filmkonserve werden den Ort später weiterverwandeln, in das Filmbild, den Filmausschnitt, der wiederum Teil einer Bildsequenz, eines Ganzen wird.

Aus Filmen und Filmbildern kann man lernen, daß die Architektur der Häuser, Straßen und Städte nicht nur ein Problem der Ordnung, der Funktion und der Wirtschaftlichkeit ist, sondern daß hier Psychologie, Atmosphäre und Bilder mitgebaut werden.

1–3. *Kino – Movie – Cinéma. 100 Jahre Film*, exhibition by the Stiftung Deutsche Kinemathek in Berlin, 1995. This exhibition was built around the first public presentation of the Marlene Dietrich estate. Architectural composition made up of ship's deck, Shanghai Express, film set and museum path by Hans Dieter Schaal.

1–3. *Kino – Movie – Cinéma. 100 Jahre Film*, Ausstellung der Stiftung Deutsche Kinemathek in Berlin, 1995. Im Mittelpunkt dieser Ausstellung stand die erste öffentliche Präsentation des Marlene-Dietrich-Nachlasses. Architektonische Komposition aus Schiffsdeck, Shanghai-Express, Film-Set und Museumsweg von Hans Dieter Schaal.

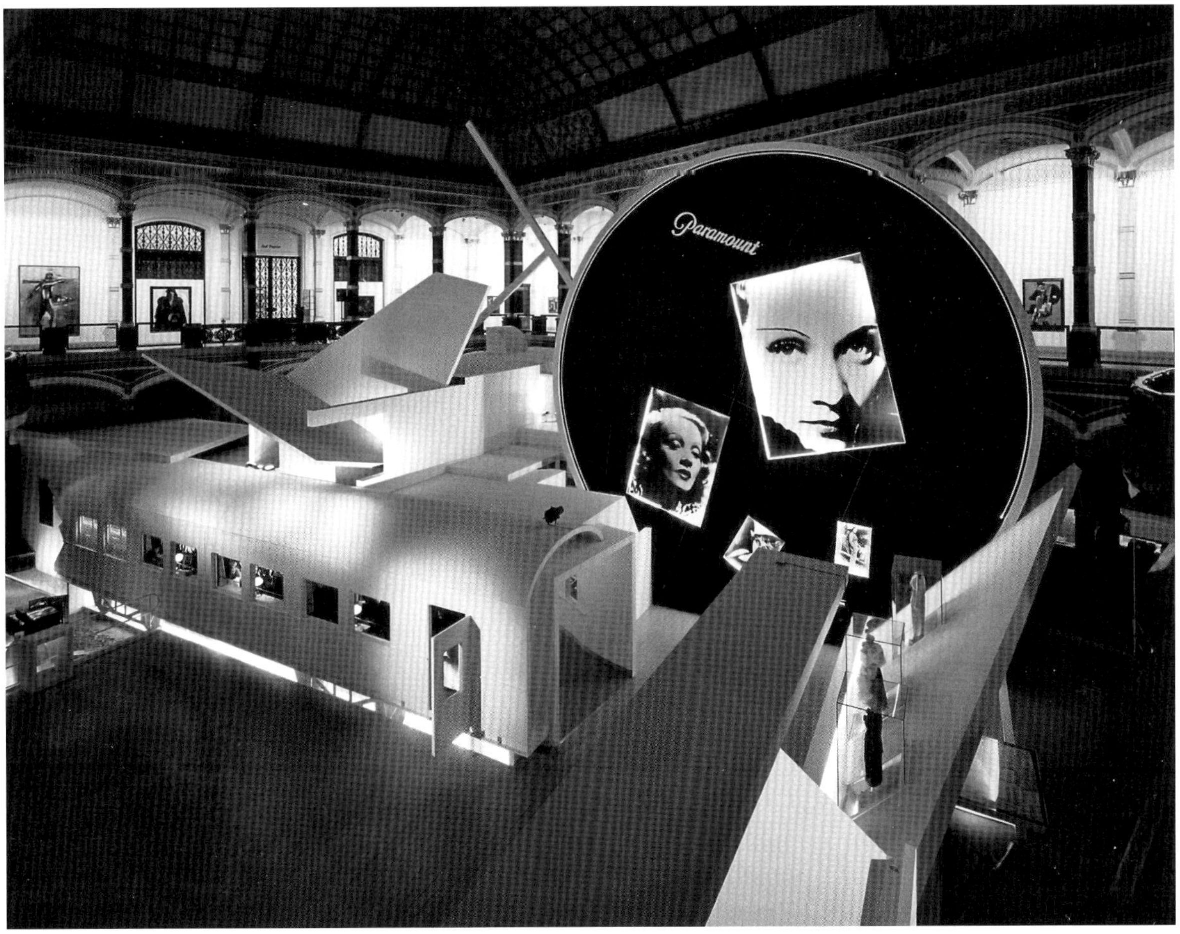

Photography and film

The advent of photography meant that for the first time in the history of mankind it was possible to make a realistic image of the world's surface through a technical medium. No discovery since writing and the printed book has more lasting influenced and changed man's social existence than photography and its consequent techniques film and television. For centuries painting was man's only depiction technique. People were familiar with the effect of the camera obscura, which could be used to project an image of the outside world into an interior, but it was not possible to fix that image. Photography marked the start of the world's being doubled into its copy. And something that was tautological in character at first – the image of reality becomes an image of reality – becomes a meaningful document in the course of time, because the illustration also reproduces a detail of time that has flowed on in the mean time. Old people can look at photographs of themselves as children. Photographs are frozen moments of a movement, taken out of the flow of time in a fraction of a second. They fulfil man's ancient longing for a moment to last for eternity, for immortality.

Because the camera lens is constructed in precisely the same way as the human eye, it depicts the visible world and space with precisely the same perspective distortion. People and things in the background are smaller than those in the foreground, and lines flow towards a distant vanishing point. As photography is a two-dimensional medium the spatial impression is merely simulated. A subjective look into space seems to be ennobled into an objective truth that can be comprehended at any time by this document that photography represents. The fiction proves the fiction. Photography makes it possible to depict everything visible. The medium has no morality and no emotional boundaries. It shows the murder victim in precisely the same way as the murderer. It shows an obscene event in just the same way as a sunset. »Photographs do not exclaim, they confirm«[1], wrote essayist Susan Sontag.

Film is a logical further development of photographic technique. The central idea was to project 24 photographs per second on to a wall so that the objects seemed to the viewer to be moving within the projection – an effect caused by the sluggishness of human perception: with this number of images per second one image can no longer be distinguished from another, the images blend with each other. The optical illusion is not perceived as such, and viewers believe that they have the real, moving world in front of them – in the image.

Filming cities and life in real time proved uninteresting from the beginning. It was more exciting to select details of this reality and stick them together in fragments and changing viewpoints. The resulting compression of space and time turned out to be the actual revolutionary feature of this completely new medium. It had previously not been known that viewers would be able to endure this kind of bombardment with splintered images and leaps in space and time, indeed even find it pleasurable.

Editing techniques, montage and collage had a powerful influence on the artistic design possibilities of fine art, painting and sculpture (Cubism, Futurism and Constructivism), on theatre, on the mood of the times, on the general way of looking at things.

It is as though the individual view had been duplicated, as though everyone's view was being shown simultaneously or in quick succession. The camera jumps and tracks from one point view to the next, as if from one ego to another. The total number of views adds up to one image, to a sequence as in a Cubist picture. Time and space are democratized and shared evenly between everybody. Every sightline is equally valid.

This depiction technique was open to manipulation from the start. Different realities and spaces could now be encapsulated within each other and blended into a unit. It was now possible to create deceptively true-looking fictions and lie perfectly with them. Long before the Surrealism of Dalí, Ernst and Magritte people and things floated over cities in Méliès' films, sewing machines turned into birds, houses, streets, cities, and people disappeared in seconds.

Film technique came at precisely the right moment. The emergence of the modern city and the development of electricity, electric light, telephones and motorized transport meant that the small-scale, static, national egocentricity of the 19th century was over. Gaps have accelerated, points of view duplicated, and Einstein's theory of relativity exploded cosmic space into minds and imaginations. Everyone was seized with giddiness and vertigo as absolute space was splintered into many space continuums with their own time, into curved spheres and black holes.

Photographie und Film

Mit der Photographie war es zum ersten Mal in der Menschheitsgeschichte möglich, die Oberfläche der Welt durch ein technisches Medium realistisch abzubilden. Keine Erfindung seit der Schrift und dem Buchdruck hat das menschliche Zusammenleben nachhaltiger beeinflußt und verändert als die Photographie mit ihren Folgetechniken, dem Film und dem Fernsehen.
Über Jahrhunderte war die Malerei die einzige Abbildtechnik des Menschen. Zwar kannte man den Effekt der Camera obscura, bei dem man das Bild der Außenwelt in einen Innenraum hineinprojizieren konnte, aber es war nicht möglich, dieses Bild zu fixieren. Mit der Photographie hatte die Verdoppelung der Welt in ihr Abbild begonnen. Und was zunächst tautologischen Charakter hatte – das Bild der Realität wird zum Bild der Realität –, wurde im Laufe der Zeit zum sinnvollen Dokument, weil die Abbildung auch einen Ausschnitt der Zeit wiedergibt, die inzwischen weitergeflossen ist. Man kann als alter Mensch das Photo von sich als Kind anschauen. Photos sind erstarrte Momente einer Bewegung, im Bruchteil einer Sekunde herausgegriffen aus dem Zeitfluß. Sie erfüllen die uralte Menschheitssehnsucht nach ewiger Dauer eines Moments, nach Unsterblichkeit.

Weil die Objektivlinse der Kamera genauso konstruiert ist wie das menschliche Auge, bildet sie die sichtbare Welt und den Raum genauso perspektivisch verzerrt ab. Die Personen und Dinge im Hintergrund sind kleiner als die im Vordergrund, die Raumlinien zielen auf einen Fluchtpunkt in der Ferne. Da die Photographie ein flächiges Medium ist, wird der Raumeindruck nur vorgetäuscht. Der subjektive Blick auf den Raum scheint durch dieses Dokument, das die Photographie darstellt, zur objektiven, jederzeit nachvollziehbaren Wahrheit geadelt. Die Fiktion beweist die Fiktion. Mit der Photographie läßt sich alles Sichtbare abbilden. Das Medium hat keine Moral und keine Gefühlsgrenzen. Sie zeigt den Ermordeten genauso wie den Mörder. Sie zeigt die obszöne Szene ebenso wie den Sonnenuntergang. »Photographien erklären nicht: sie bestätigen«[1], schrieb die Essayistin Susan Sontag.

Der Film ist eine konsequente Weiterentwicklung der photographischen Technik. Die zentrale Idee bestand darin, 24 Photos in der Sekunde an die Wand zu projizieren, so daß sich für den Betrachter die Objekte innerhalb der Projektion zu bewegen scheinen – ein Effekt, der aus der Trägheit der menschlichen Wahrnehmung resultiert: Bei dieser Bilderanzahl in der Sekunde läßt sich das eine Bild nicht mehr von dem anderen unterscheiden. Man nimmt die optische Täuschung nicht als solche wahr und glaubt die reale, bewegte Welt vor sich zu haben.

Die Abfilmung von Stadt und Leben in Realzeit erwies sich von Anfang an als uninteressant. Spannender war es, Ausschnitte aus dieser Realität in Fragmenten und wechselnden Blickrichtungen aneinanderzukleben. Die so entstehende Komprimierung von Raum und Zeit stellte sich als das eigentlich Revolutionäre dieses vollkommen neuen Mediums heraus. Bisher hatte man nicht gewußt, daß der Zuschauer ein solches Bombardement aus Bildsplittern, Raum- und Zeitsprüngen überhaupt ertragen würde, ja sogar Vergnügen daran haben könnte.

Als künstlerische Gestaltungsmöglichkeiten hatten die Schnittechnik, die Montage und die Collage einen starken Einfluß auf die bildende Kunst, auf Malerei und Bildhauerei (Kubismus, Futurismus und Konstruktivismus), auf das Theater, auf die Zeitstimmung, auf das allgemeine Sehverhalten. Es ist, als sei der Blick des Einzelnen vervielfältigt worden, als würden gleichzeitig oder dicht hintereinander die Blicke aller Menschen gezeigt. Die Kamera springt und fährt von einem Standpunkt zum nächsten, wie von einem Ich zum anderen. Die Gesamtanzahl der Blicke addiert sich zu einem Bild, zu einer Sequenz wie im kubistischen Bild. Raum und Zeit werden demokratisiert und gleichmäßig auf alle verteilt. Jede Blickrichtung ist gleichberechtigt.

Natürlich war diese Abbildtechnik von Anfang an auch manipulierbar. Man konnte nun verschiedene Realitäten und Räume ineinander verschachteln, sie zu einer Einheit verschmelzen. Man konnte nun täuschend wahr aussehende Fiktionen herstellen und damit perfekt lügen. Lange vor dem Surrealismus von Dalí, Ernst und Magritte schwebten in den Filmen von Méliès die Menschen und Dinge über den Städten, verwandelten sich Nähmaschinen in Vögel, verschwanden in Sekunden Häuser, Straßen, Städte und Menschen.

Die Technik des Films kam genau zum richtigen Zeitpunkt. Mit der Entstehung der modernen Großstadt und der Entwicklung von Elektrizität, Glühbirne, Telephon und Autoverkehr war es vorbei mit der kleinräumigen, statischen, nationalen Ichbezogenheit des 19. Jahrhunderts. Die Zwischenräume haben sich beschleunigt, die Gesichtspunkte vervielfältigt, und der kosmische Raum explodierte mit Einsteins Relativitätstheorie in den Köpfen und Vorstellungen. Taumel und Schwindelgefühl erfaßte alle Menschen bei der Aufsplitterung des absoluten Raums in viele Raumkontinuen mit Eigenzeiten, in gekrümmte Sphären und schwarze Löcher.

Spiritual spaces

Film architecture – interiors and exteriors – is always architecture that has been depicted, photographed, turned into an image. It embraces the actors and scenes like an air-space that has become visible, like a built coat, a petrified robe, a stage set. Its presence defines the setting, the social position of the characters and their inner mood. The openings in the walls and ceilings, the windows, doors and slits, determine the geometry of incident light. Visible light sources complete the picture. Film architecture is fictional architecture. It is unimportant whether a city, a building, a room exist in reality or whether only the façades have been built up. Film architecture is an architecture of meaning.[2] There is nothing in the frame that is not important and does not have something to say. Of course this architecture is constructed and its importance appreciated only for the short moment of being filmed, after that it is in the way, and rots away as a tiresome ruin or is taken down, unless it becomes part of a studio tour. It lives its true life in the film, as a new, atmospheric truth. Camera and film have transformed it from studio reality into media fiction. Film architecture works in statements and images, with built psychology, spiritual spaces, spiritual landscapes. Film space is an emotional place made up of walls, light and shade. The more intense, brilliant and melancholic the atmosphere becomes, the more powerful is its effect in the film. This unity of mood between character and place has been sought from the very beginning. German Expressionist films were the great pioneers here – even if on a somewhat exaggerated plane – and made world-wide impact with their work. The heroes of these films, threatened from inside and out, often mad, and communicating by means of supernatural powers, roam with the exalted gestures of silent film through a labyrinth of narrow alleys that can represent both a medieval city and a spiritual space that has become visible.

City, house, room, chamber, street, alley – every motif is demonized and related directly to the characters involved as a psychological element. These characters were seized by panic fear as buildings crashed down on them, and saw personal deaths on steps and in alleyways. The built labyrinth wrapped itself round their necks and killed them. What Expressionist pictures had formulated before them (Ludwig Meidner and Ernst Ludwig Kirchner) was realized as a moving film image in *The Cabinet of Dr. Caligari* (1919/20). The effect of an oil painting hanging in a museum was far exceeded here in the cinema's black box. People saw their own nightmares in the projected image at the end of the tunnel, unreality breaking into the waking consciousness in a way that was almost real. The film – and thus its architecture – had arrived at the core of its own effectiveness: a day-dream become image, day-dream space become image, with all the magic of an archetypal spell, a sober intoxication, a fictitious journey through world, city, life and ego. And also a journey through time and space with picture-stories of childhood, feelings, despair, love and hate, adventure, danger and death. An easy death in the cinema gives the viewer in the darkened cinema the divine feeling of being immortal, able to step out into the night as a survivor.

All subsequent film spaces and film architecture developed from the Expressionist space-cell with its atmosphere of actors, mood of the times, social status, level of consciousness, of face, body, architecture and light fused into pictorial unity. There are elements of this inside-outside inversion in French films by Marcel Carné and René Clair, in the Hollywood Black Series and the films of Alfred Hitchcock, in Billy Wilder and in early films by Luchino Visconti and Federico Fellini, in Ingmar Bergman's and Woody Allen's films. Every great film director tried to create this unity. And this often means that the chosen space, the building or the city becomes the leading character in the film: *The Cabinet of Dr. Caligari, Metropolis, Key Largo, Sunset Boulevard, The Silence, Viridiana, Manhattan, Roma, Subway, Batman, Psycho, Shadow of a Doubt, Rear Window, Notorious, Rebecca, The Blue Angel, The Last Laugh, King Kong, Blade Runner, Pulp Fiction.*

Films set in front of an empty white wall, in non-places, are scarcely conceivable. Space and architecture have always to be firmly established within the landscape, the city and the real or fictitious society. Where the story is set is crucial: on a skyscraper, in a house in a village, a castle, a palace, an ordinary home, at the bottom of the sea or in outer space, detached from everything.

Seelenräume

Die Architektur des Films – die Innen- und die Außenräume – ist immer eine abgebildete, abphotographierte, zum Bild gewordene Architektur. Sie umgreift die handelnden Schauspieler und die Szenen wie ein sichtbar gewordener Luftraum, wie ein gebauter Mantel, ein versteinertes Kleid, ein Bühnenbild. Sie bestimmt den Ort der Handlung, die gesellschaftliche Stellung der Personen und deren innere Stimmung. Die Öffnungen der Wände und Decken, die Fenster, Türen und Schlitze, legen die Geometrie der Lichteinfälle fest. Sichtbare Lichtquellen ergänzen das Bild. Die Architektur des Films ist eine Architektur der Fiktion. Es ist unwichtig, ob eine Stadt, ein Haus, ein Raum real existieren oder ob nur die Fassaden aufgebaut worden sind. Filmarchitektur ist Bedeutungsarchitektur.[2] Innerhalb des Bildausschnitts gibt es nichts, was nicht wichtig wäre und mitspräche. Allerdings wird diese Architektur nur für den kurzen Moment des Abgefilmtwerdens aufgebaut und in ihrer Bedeutung gewürdigt, danach steht sie im Weg, zerfällt als lästige Ruine, oder man reißt sie ab, es sei denn, sie wird zur Station einer Studiotour. Im Film lebt sie als neue, stimmungsvolle Wahrheit ihr wahres Leben. Sie ist mit Kamera und Film aus der Studiorealität in eine mediale Fiktion verwandelt worden. Filmarchitekturen sind Aussage- und Bildarchitekturen, gebaute Psychologien, Seelenräume, Seelenlandschaften. Der Filmraum ist ein emotionaler Ort aus Wänden, aus Licht und Schatten. Je intensiver, glänzender und melancholischer die Raumatmosphäre, desto stärker die Bildwirkung im Film. Von Anfang an wurde diese Einheit von Stimmung der Person und Stimmung des Ortes angestrebt. Es war vor allem der deutsche expressionistische Film, der hier – wenn auch übertriebene – Pioniertaten vollbrachte und damit eine weltweite Wirkung erzielte. Die innen und außen bedrohten, oft geisteskranken, mit übernatürlichen Kräften kommunizierenden Helden irren mit exaltierter Stummfilmgestik durch ein Gassenlabyrinth, das sowohl eine mittelalterliche Stadt als auch einen sichtbar gewordenen Seelenraum darstellen kann.

Stadt, Haus, Zimmer, Kammer, Straße, Gasse – jedes Motiv wurde dämonisiert und als psychologisches Moment direkt auf die handelnden Personen bezogen. In panischer Angst sahen diese die Fassaden auf sich niederstürzen, erblickten in Treppen und Gängen persönliche Todesfallen. Das gebaute Labyrinth schnürte sich um ihren Hals und brachte sie um. Was in den expressionistischen Bildern vorformuliert worden war (Ludwig Meidner und Ernst Ludwig Kirchner), wurde zum Beispiel im *Cabinet des Dr. Caligari* (1919/20) im bewegten Filmbild realisiert. Die Wirkung eines im Museum aufgehängten Ölbilds wurde hier in der schwarzen Kiste des Kinos weit übertroffen. Man sah am Ende des Tunnels im projizierten Lichtbild den eigenen Angsttraum, das fast reale Hereinbrechen des Unwirklichen in das hellwache Bewußtsein. Der Film – und damit seine Architekturen – war im Kernbereich seiner eigentlichen Wirkung angekommen: bildgewordener Tagtraum, bildgewordener Tagtraumraum mit der Magie eines archetypischen Zaubers, eines nüchternen Rauschs, einer fiktiven Reise durch Welt, Stadt, Leben und Ich. Auch eine Reise durch Raum und Zeit mit Bildergeschichten von Kindheiten, Gefühlen, Verzweiflungen, von Liebe und Haß, von Abenteuer, Gefahren und Tod. Das leichte Sterben im Kino vermittelt dem Zuschauer im dunklen Kinosaal das göttliche Gefühl, unsterblich zu sein und als Überlebender hinaustreten zu können auf die nächtliche Straße.

Aus der expressionistischen Raumzelle mit ihrer zur Bildeinheit verschmolzenen Atmosphäre aus Schauspieler, Zeitstimmung, Gesellschaftsstand, Bewußtseinsgrad, aus Gesicht, Körper, Architektur und Licht entwickelten sich alle folgenden Filmräume und Filmarchitekturen. Man findet Elemente dieser Innen-Außen-Verkehrung in den französischen Filmen von Marcel Carné und René Clair genauso wie in der Schwarzen Serie Hollywoods und in den Filmen Alfred Hitchcocks, bei Billy Wilder ebenso wie in den frühen Filmen von Luchino Visconti und Federico Fellini, in den Filmen Ingmar Bergmans und Woody Allens. Jeder große Filmregisseur versuchte, diese Einheit herzustellen. Dabei kommt es immer wieder vor, daß der gewählte Raum, das Haus oder die Stadt zur Hauptperson des Films wird: *Das Cabinet des Dr. Caligari, Metropolis, Hafen des Lasters / Gangster vor Key Largo, Boulevard der Dämmerung, Das Schweigen, Viridiana, Manhattan, Fellinis Roma, Subway, Batman, Psycho, Im Schatten des Zweifels, Das Fenster zum Hof, Weißes Gift / Berüchtigt, Rebekka, Der blaue Engel, Der letzte Mann, King-Kong und die weiße Frau, Blade Runner, Pulp Fiction.*

Filme vor leerer, weißer Wand, an Nicht-Orten sind kaum vorstellbar. Raum und Architektur müssen fest in die Landschaft, die Stadt und die reale oder fiktive Gesellschaft eingebaut sein. Entscheidend ist, wo die Geschichte spielt: auf einem Wolkenkratzer, in einem Dorfhaus, in einer Burg, einem Schloß, einer Bürgerwohnung, am Grund des Meeres oder losgelöst von allem im Weltall.

Architecture as built expression: soul landscapes and soul places.
4, 5. *The Cabinet of Dr. Caligari,* 1919/20; director: Robert Wiene, architecture: Walter Reimann, Walter Röhrig and Hermann Warm.
6. *Genuine*, 1920; director: Robert Wiene, architecture: César Klein with Bernhard Klein and Kurt Hermann Rosenberg.

Architektur als gebaute Expression: Seelenlandschaften und Seelenräume.
4, 5. *Das Cabinet des Dr. Caligari,* 1919/20; Regie: Robert Wiene, Architektur: Walter Reimann, Walter Röhrig und Hermann Warm.
6. *Genuine*, 1920; Regie: Robert Wiene, Architektur: César Klein mit Bernhard Klein und Kurt Hermann Rosenberg.

Metropolis (1925/26), for example, is the first film in which the modern city is the leading character. There had been films about »cities« before it, like *The Golem* (1920) with Hans Poelzig's Expressionist-Romantic architecture or *Faust* (1925/26) by Friedrich Wilhelm Murnau (city from above). But it was never a large modern city that was shown here, but the medieval town, with its narrow alleys and crooked half-timbered houses. The film was dreaming backwards. These fictions drew their images from what once had been. The fact that the buildings were even more like a fairy-tale and more developed than they were in reality was derived from the film-makers' subjective and poetic eye. They built in the world of their own desires and childhood. There is probably no film about which so much has been written as *Metropolis*. Despite the questionably kitschy plot it is and remains the most fascinating architectural film there is. It does not glorify the city, but presents it as a voracious giant that eats and represses everything, from whom there is no escape. The narrow medieval alleys of the Expressionist film have become gigantic canyons with traffic streaming through them ceaselessly. A vertical urban structure: the caves of the lower city are dominated by dull obedience, mass slavery. Above this is the city of machines and the bourgeoisie, and on the highest plane – in the tops of the skyscrapers – the rulers reside, with their paradisal interiors.

Utopian antiquity, the skyscraper as a galley with machines. Man has imprisoned himself in a self-built anthill. Piranesi's nightmares have become film reality. Fear gives birth to monsters. A prison within a prison: the machine wreckers are shut in as well. The disaster can no longer be averted. Metropolis is the Nibelung's castle grown to gigantic proportions, fully automated and technological, with the cellar vaults of the lower city as steel caves and death-bringing bunker catacombs and the skyscrapers as pyramids of power and oppression.

The film's gigantomania is its revolutionary quality. Little worries in narrow alleys are not interesting any more: attention is turned to a view of urban catastrophe.

The city is also an elemental subject in *King Kong* (1933) by Cooper and Schoedsack.

A giant gorilla is discovered and captured by a film crew on a remote island. It is taken by sea to Manhattan and presented there as a world sensation in theatres. Thanks to its enormous strength the animal is finally able to escape. It abducts a beautiful woman whom it finds affecting and takes refuge on top of what was then the world's highest building, the Empire State Building. It ends in the famous melodramatic showdown at the top of the skyscraper: Aeroplanes circle round the animal, with soldiers in their cockpits firing at it. The gorilla is still holding the woman in his paw, but then he puts her down on a ledge and tries to grab the aeroplanes. He succeeds once. But finally the massive body is so riddled with bullets that King Kong loses his firm grip on the skyscraper's aerial, sways and crashes backwards into the depths of the street canyons. In the final shot we see the gigantic animal's dead body lying on the asphalt, with a crowd of people staring at it. The last two sentences spoken in the film are: »It wasn't the airplanes. It was Beauty killed the Beast.« The End.

Civilization has won, but it was briefly in danger and confronted with the primeval force of wild nature. This force lies buried under Manhattan. Civilization has forced out the jungle.

The Empire State Building is still standing, no longer the world's tallest building, but is has defied all danger, even when an American fighter plane crashed into it in the Second World War and turned the 79th floor into a chaotic inferno, with 14 dead and 25 seriously injured. One of the plane's engines even burst through the rear façade and fell on a neighbouring building, setting it on fire. Later incidents of this kind provided material for Hollywood's nightmarish disaster movies.

The city was also the central theme of Hollywood's Black Series, starting with Orson Welles' *Citizen Kane* (1940/41) and *The Maltese Falcon* (1941), John Huston's first feature film, and extending into the fifties.The theme had previously been formulated in Fritz Lang's and Robert Siodmak's films, *M* for instance. In contrast with *Metropolis*, the city scarcely ever appears as a physical figure, apart from a few long shots in the opening sequence. Most of the scenes are played in dark back rooms, in pubs, cellars, in sleazy hotels and outside obscure front doors. Although the city is the omnipresent theme, as prison, hiding-place or jungle, it appears only indirectly, in scraps of conversation, and the names of streets and places. In a sense we see only the rear side of the town, a forgotten shady area. The characters do not care whether there are skyscrapers towering over them or only five-storey buildings, all the confusion takes place in a labyrinth of grey walls and dark intrigue. This fragmentation of the city and refusal to let it be seen in its totality is the strange new quality of these films. As they are set almost entirely at night, their visible presence is all but extinguished – scenes where incidents take place are lit only by scant pools of light. The melancholy of failure hangs over everything. Crimes are always being committed, one gang is always after another, and the end is always tragic.

In *The Asphalt Jungle* (1950) the city becomes an underwater jungle in which people can hide and in which safes full of valuable jewels gleam. Subterranean corridor systems lead to the bank's cellar wall. The group breaks through this wall, disarms the electronic security system and blows up the safe. All four men involved in the raid are dreaming of big money, of a life in Mexico in the country in the bosom of the family. This dream will come true for none of them, and they are killed one by one. The last of the four crooks dies in the final shot in the middle of a paddock in the open countryside. Horses come right up to the dying man and look at him uncomprehendingly. An alien interloper into their peaceful world.

This final shot brings the subject-matter of the Black Films completely to a head: anyone who has got mixed up with the city, who is dazzled by its inner brilliance, its wealth, its power and its sex will never get away from it – is addicted, with no hope of a cure. And anyone who tries to break off the struggle for advancement and victory by running away will be destroyed. There is no escape from the asphalt jungle. The price of waking up in the open countryside is always death.

The city is chaos, sin, perversion, entanglement, addiction, crime, the police, an abyss for many, and a place of happiness and advancement for few. The city is a trap. One of the basic threats within the mirrored labyrinth of the city is losing one's own ego, one's individuality. Alfred Hitchcock addressed this problem in his film *The Wrong Man* (1956): a harmless musician who plays bass every evening in a night club, and who has a beautiful wife and two sons, and lives in a little suburban terraced house, is suspected of being a robber one day, and arrested. It is really a case of mistaken identity, but all the evidence is against him. He has to spend a night in prison and survive a depressing trial which he finally wins because the real culprit has committed another robbery and been caught.

As the plot proceeds the city transforms itself into a system that turns against an innocent citizen. The cage-like cell in the prison becomes an extreme counter-image of his own little house. The city contains both possibilities. The film shows how quickly things can be reversed.

Once more state of mind and the external architectural image are equated. Inside becomes outside. Outside inside. Mirror worlds. It is not surprising that real mirrors are often placed in the rooms. The protagonists see themselves in the mirror, are confronted with their present gloomy psychological condition and thus finally blend in with the room. Rooms within rooms are created, open to experience for the audience and the protagonists, motifs of entanglement, of the labyrinthine become image. For a moment people are really captured in a reflection as in a picture, a frozen photographic space.

All the films described so far are in black and white. Physical fusion with the surrounding space is possible only in this colourless condition. Colour distracts, approaches the infinite multiplicity of reality. It is only by restricting and stylizing that the degree of concentration can be achieved that the film image and film architecture need to develop their full mood atmosphere and effect.

In films as in reality the city is an embodiment of today for its occupants and users, absolutely now, absolutely present – but it can also be desired object in the past, the future or the distance. The most important city film after *Metropolis*, even though the city hardly appears in it, but is an exotic place to which to escape, is Michael Curtiz's *Casablanca* (1942).

The film takes place under the Third Reich. Half Europe is occupied by the Nazis, who are seizing power in an ever-increasing number of countries. Casablanca, the white port in North Africa, is the last hope for many people. It is possible to get a visa for America here, with money, bribery and intrigue. People live in small hotels and sleazy boarding houses, rarely jostling through the crowded alleys and preferring to spend time in the »Blue Parrot« or »Rick's American Café«. This is where all paths cross, where negotiations about visas happen, and where arrangements about departure are made. Nobody really gets involved in this city, no-one wants to live here completely. Casablanca is just a place to pass through, and everyone wants to leave it as quickly as possible. Only hardened cynics like Rick (Humphrey Bogart) and the Prefect of Police (Claude Rains) stay here for longer. The story is well known: Ilsa Lund (Ingrid Bergman) appears in Rick's café one day – a long-past Paris love story, as it turns out. Major emotions begin to accumulate. Alcohol, threats, hopes. Ilsa has married. The end is familiar: the famous scene at the airport: »I'm looking into your eyes, little one.« Just a quick murder at the German commandant's headquarters and the usual suspects are arrested. As we know, the start of a great friendship between Rick and the chief of police. The fact that the city remains uneasy to the end – the final scene plays in dense fog – makes the place doubly mysterious. It is not the picturesque tourist elements that are interesting, and not the exoticism either – that is just an alarming accessory – but private fates against a backdrop of history. Every city is the same, cynics would say, sometimes you're in Paris, sometimes in New York. What matters for Rick is personal manœuvre and whisky.

Putting together plot, characters and architecture to make a film image produces combinations that are fixed for all time: city becomes image, not as such, but always in the context of a story. Urban films explain cities and encode them at the same time. They offer perspectives and ways of looking at things from a certain human position on each occasion: the persecuted experience the city differently from their persecutors, lonely people differently from lovers, schoolboys differently from old men.

Urban films are always about possibilities. The degree of pragmatism or Utopia they provide develops from their plot. Today negative urban visions prevail; using the city comfortably, in the way we saw in French films of the thirties, forties and fifties no longer counts, where all kinds of people and lifestyles could develop alongside each other with equal status – for example in René Clair's *Under the Roofs of Paris* (1930) or *Gates of Paris* (1957), also by René Clair, and in the films of Marcel Carné and Jacques Tati.

There the city (Paris in particular) was still the motherly covering that put up with everything forbearingly, gave everyone a glass of red wine and a place at the bar. The urban romanticism of Fellini's *I Vitelloni* (1953) is also a thing of the past. Woody Allen comes closest to maintaining a slightly transfigured view of metropolis New York (*Manhattan*, 1979), urban disasters have shifted into his psyche and city-dwellers get on each other's nerves with their aggressive neuroses. Violence predominates: *Subway* (1985), *Pulp Fiction* (1994). The view of the future is gloomy as well. The Science Fiction cities that have developed out of *Metropolis* are even more like prisons than their predecessors. Total surveillance mechanisms are in place. There can be no more escape: *Blade Runner* (1982), *Batman* (1989).

This development reflects real conditions, above all in American cities. A quiet life is possible only within fenced ghettos with video security systems. Anyone who risks going out into the street at night in Los Angeles, for example, is in deadly danger. Gangs dominate the scene. Every pedestrian and every motorist is fair game. A latent civil war.

Pedestrian areas in European cities have also become potential scenes of crime. Their nocturnal emptiness is a premonition of hell. The future will be all the more gloomy. Films provide a picture of this.

Städte

Metropolis (1925/26) zum Beispiel ist der erste Film, in dem die moderne Großstadt die Hauptrolle spielt. Davor gab es auch schon Filme, die sich mit dem Thema »Stadt« befaßten, wie etwa *Der Golem, wie er in die Welt kam* (1920) mit den romantisch-expressionistischen Architekturen von Hans Poelzig oder *Faust* (1925/26) von Friedrich Wilhelm Murnau (Stadt von oben). Es war aber nie die moderne Großstadt, die dabei ins Bild rückte, sondern die mittelalterliche Stadt, mit ihren engen Gassen und krummen Fachwerkhäusern. Der Film träumte rückwärts. Die Fiktionen schöpften ihre Bilder aus dem, was einmal war. Daß dabei die Häuser noch märchenhafter und gewachsener erschienen, als sie in Wirklichkeit waren, entsprang dem subjektiv-poetischen Blick der Filmarchitekten. Man baute seine eigene Wunsch- und Kindheitswelt mit hinein. Wahrscheinlich ist über keinen Film mehr geschrieben worden als über *Metropolis.* Bei aller Fragwürdigkeit der kitschigen Handlung ist und bleibt er der faszinierendste Architekturfilm, den es gibt. Er verherrlicht die Großstadt nicht, sondern schildert sie als alles fressenden und alles unterdrückenden Moloch, vor dem es kein Entrinnen gibt. Die engen mittelalterlichen Gassen des expressionistischen Films sind zu gigantischen Cañyons geworden, durch die der Verkehr unaufhörlich strömt. Eine vertikale Stadtstruktur: In den Höhlen der Unterstadt herrscht dumpfer Gehorsam, massenhaftes Sklaventum. Darüber gibt es die Maschinen- und die Bürgerstadt, und auf der höchsten Ebene – in den Spitzen der Wolkenkratzer – liegt die Residenz der Herrscher mit paradiesischen Interieurs.

Utopische Antike, der Wolkenkratzer als Maschinengaleere. Der Mensch hat sich in seinem selbstgebauten Termitengebirge gefangengesetzt. Piranesis Alpträume sind Filmwirklichkeit geworden. Die Angst gebiert Ungeheuer. Gefängnis im Gefängnis: Auch die Maschinenstürmer werden eingemauert. Der Lauf des Unheils läßt sich nicht mehr aufhalten. Metropolis, das ist die ins Gigantische angewachsene, vollautomatisierte, technische Nibelungenburg mit den Kellergewölben der Unterstadt als Stahlhöhlen und todbringenden Bunkerkatakomben und den Wolkenkratzertürmen als Macht- und Unterdrückungspyramiden.

Die Gigantomanie des Films ist das Revolutionäre an ihm. Nicht mehr die kleinen Sorgen in den engen Gassen interessieren, sondern der Blick auf die urbane Katastrophe.

Auch in *King-Kong und die weiße Frau* (1933) von Cooper und Schoedsack ist die Großstadt in elementarer Weise thematisiert worden.

Ein Riesengorilla wird von einer Filmcrew auf einer abgelegenen Insel aufgespürt und gefangengenommen. Man bringt ihn mit dem Schiff nach Manhattan und führt ihn dort als Weltsensation in Theatern vor. Dank seiner enormen Kraft gelingt es dem Tier schließlich, zu entkommen. Es flieht mit einer entführten schönen Frau, für die es Gefühle empfindet, auf das damals höchste Gebäude der Welt, das Empire State Building. Es kommt zu dem berühmten melodramatischen Showdown auf der Spitze des Wolkenkratzers: Flugzeuge umkreisen das Tier, in den Cockpits sitzen Soldaten an Maschinengewehren und feuern auf das Riesentier. Noch hält der Gorilla die Frau in seiner Pratze, doch dann legt er sie auf einem Mauervorsprung ab und versucht, die Flugzeuge aus der Luft zu greifen. Einmal gelingt es ihm. Schließlich jedoch ist der gewaltige Leib so von Kugeln durchsiebt, daß King-Kong den festen Griff um die Wolkenkratzer-Antenne lockert, taumelt und rückwärts in die Tiefe der Straßenschluchten stürzt. Im Schlußbild sieht man den riesigen toten Tierkörper auf dem Asphalt liegen, von einer Menschenmenge begafft. Die zwei letzten gesprochenen Sätze des Films lauten: »Die Flieger haben ihn geschafft.« »Nein, er hat das Mädel zu sehr geliebt.« Ende.

Die Zivilisation hat gesiegt, aber sie war für kurze Zeit gefährdet und mit der Urkraft der wilden Natur konfrontiert. Diese Kraft liegt unter Manhattan begraben. Die Zivilisation hat den Urwald verdrängt.

Das Empire State Building steht heute immer noch, es ist zwar nicht mehr das höchste Gebäude der Welt, aber es hat allen Gefahren getrotzt, auch dem Aufprall eines US-Kampfflugzeugs während des Zweiten Weltkriegs, das das 79. Stockwerk in ein brennendes Chaos verwandelte mit 14 Toten und 25 Schwerverletzten. Einer der Flugzeugmotoren durchschlug sogar die Rückfassade und fiel auf ein benachbartes Haus, das dadurch in Brand geriet. Später wurde aus solchen Vorfällen der Stoff für die alptraumhaften Katastrophenfilme Hollywoods.

Die Großstadt war auch das zentrale Thema der Schwarzen Serie Hollywoods, die mit Orson Welles' *Citizen Kane* (1940/41) und *Die Spur des Falken* (1941), dem Spielfilmdebüt von John Huston, begann und bis in die fünfziger Jahre hinein reichte, vorformuliert durch die Filme Fritz Langs und Robert Siodmaks, zum Beispiel *M – Eine Stadt sucht einen Mörder*. Im Gegensatz zu *Metropolis* taucht die Stadt in ihrer physischen Gestalt so gut wie überhaupt nicht auf, wenn man von einigen Totalen in der Eingangssequenz absieht. Die meisten Szenen spielen in dunklen Hinterzimmern, in Kneipen, Kellern, in vergammelten Absteigen und vor abgelegenen Eingangstüren. Obwohl die Stadt das alles beherrschende Thema ist – Gefängnis, Versteck oder Dschungel –, erscheint sie nur indirekt, in Gesprächsfetzen und Bezeichnungen von Straßen und Orten. In gewisser Weise sieht man die Rückseite der Stadt, den vergessenen Schattenbereich. Es ist den Figuren gleichgültig, ob sich über ihnen Wolkenkratzertürmen oder nur fünfgeschossige Häuser, die Verwirrung findet in einem Labyrinth aus grauen Wänden und dunklen Intrigen statt. Diese Fragmentierung der Großstadt und die Verweigerung, sie in ihrer Totalität ins Bild zu rücken, ist das eigenartig Neue an diesen Filmen. Da sie fast ausschließlich nachts spielen, liegt die Auslöschung ihrer sichtbaren Anwesenheit nahe – nur karge Lichtinseln beleuchten die Tatorte. Die Melancholie des Scheiterns liegt über allem. Immer wird ein Verbrechen begangen, immer jagt eine Gruppe die andere, und immer endet die Handlung tragisch.

In *Asphalt Dschungel* (1950) wird die Stadt zum Unterwasserdickicht, in dem man sich versteckt und in dem die Tresore mit den wertvollen Juwelenschätzen glänzen. Durch unterirdische Gangsysteme gelangt man zur Kellerwand der Bank. Man durchbricht diese Wand, überwindet die elektronischen Sicherungsanlagen und sprengt den Tresor. Alle vier am Coup Beteiligten träumen vom großen Geld, von einem Leben in Mexiko, auf dem Lande und in trauter Familie. Alle vier werden den Traum nicht erleben und nacheinander ihren Tod finden. Der letzte der vier Ganoven stirbt im Schlußbild mitten auf einer Pferdekoppel in freier Landschaft. Die Pferde kommen ganz nah an den Sterbenden heran und betrachten ihn verständnislos. Ein fremder Eindringling in ihre friedliche Welt.

Dieses Schlußbild bringt noch einmal die ganze Thematik der schwarzen Stadtfilme auf den Punkt: Wer sich mit der Stadt eingelassen hat, wer von ihrem inneren Glanz, ihrem Reichtum, ihrer Macht, ihrem Sex einmal geblendet worden ist, kommt nicht mehr von ihr los – ist ein Süchtiger, ohne Aussicht auf Heilung. Und wer den Kampf um den Aufstieg und um den Sieg abbrechen will und der Stadt entflieht, geht kaputt. Es gibt kein Entkommen aus dem Asphaltdschungel. Jedes Erwachen in der freien Landschaft wird mit dem Tod bezahlt.

Stadt ist das Chaos, die Sünde, die Perversion, die Verstrickung, die Sucht, das Verbrechen, die Polizei, Abgrund für viele, Bereich des Glücks und des Aufstiegs für wenige. Stadt ist die Falle. Eine Grundbedrohung innerhalb des Spiegellabyrinths der Großstadt ist der Verlust des eigenen Ichs, der Individualität. In dem Film *Der falsche Mann* (1956) hat Alfred Hitchcock dieses Problem thematisiert: Ein harmloser Musiker, der jeden Abend Baß in einem Nachtclub spielt, der eine schöne Frau und zwei kleine Söhne hat, der ein kleines Reihenhäuschen im Vorort bewohnt, wird eines Tages als Räuber verdächtigt und verhaftet. In Wirklichkeit liegt eine Verwechslung vor, aber alle Indizien sprechen gegen ihn. Er muß eine Nacht im Gefängnis verbringen und einen deprimierenden Prozeß überstehen, den er schließlich als Gewinner verlassen kann, weil der wahre Täter wieder einen Überfall verübt hat und gefaßt worden ist.

Im Verlauf der Handlung verwandelt sich die Stadt in ein System, das sich gegen einen unschuldigen Bürger wendet. Die käfigartige Zelle im Gefängnis wird zum äußersten Gegenbild seines eigenen Häuschens. Beide Möglichkeiten stecken in der Stadt. Der Film zeigt, wie schnell sich ein Seitenwechsel vollziehen kann.

Wieder ist die Gleichsetzung von innerer Befindlichkeit und äußerem Architekturbild erreicht. Innen wird außen. Außen innen. Spiegelwelten. Es verwundert nicht, daß tatsächlich oft Spiegel im Raum eingesetzt werden. Die Handelnden sehen sich selbst darin, werden mit ihrem gegenwärtigen dunklen, psychischen Zustand konfrontiert und verschmelzen so endgültig mit dem Raum. Es entstehen Räume im Raum, für den Zuschauer erlebbar und für die Handelnden. Außerdem sind sie Motive der Verstrickung, des bildgewordenen Labyrinthischen. Im Spiegelbild ist man für Momente tatsächlich gefangen wie in einem Bild, einem erstarrten Photoraum.

Alle bisher beschriebenen Filme sind Schwarzweißfilme. Nur in diesem farblosen Zustand ist die psychische Verschmelzung ganz zu schaffen. Farbe lenkt ab, nähert sich der unendlichen Vielfalt der Realität. Nur in der Beschränkung und Stilisierung ist der Grad an Konzentration zu erreichen, den das Filmbild und die Filmarchitektur brauchen, um sich in ihrer Stimmung, ihrer Atmosphäre und ihrer Wirkung ganz entfalten zu können.

Stadt ist im Film wie in Wirklichkeit für ihre Bewohner und Benutzer das verkörperte Heute, ganz jetzt, ganz Gegenwart – aber sie kann auch das Objekt der Sehnsucht in der Vergangenheit, in der Zukunft oder in der Ferne sein. Der nach *Metropolis* berühmteste Stadtfilm, in dem allerdings die Stadt kaum vorkommt und zum exotisch fremden Fluchtpunkt wird, zum Tor der Freiheit, ist *Casablanca* (1942) von Michael Curtiz.

Der Film spielt während des Dritten Reiches. Halb Europa ist von den Nazis besetzt, die in immer mehr Ländern der Welt nach der Macht greifen. Casablanca, die weiße Hafenstadt in Nordafrika, wird für viele Flüchtende zur letzten Hoffnung. Von hier gibt es noch die Möglichkeit, mit Geld, Bestechung und Intrige, ein Visum nach Amerika zu erhalten. Man wohnt in kleinen Hotels und Absteigen, überquert nur kurz die überfüllten Gassen und hält sich vor allem im »Blauen Papagei« oder in »Ricks Café Américain« auf. Hier kreuzen sich die Wege, hier wird über die Visa verhandelt, hier werden die Verabredungen zur Abreise getroffen. Niemand nimmt diese Stadt wirklich wahr, niemand will hier ganz leben. Casablanca ist der Durchgangsort, den man so schnell wie möglich verlassen will. Nur die harten Zyniker wie Rick (Humphrey Bogart) und den Polizeipräfekten (Claude Rains) hält es hier länger. Man kennt die Geschichte: Ilsa Lund (Ingrid Bergman) erscheint eines Tages in Ricks Café, eine alte, große Liebesgeschichte aus Pariser Tagen, wie sich herausstellt. Große Gefühle türmen sich auf. Alkohol, Bedrohungen, Hoffnungen. Ilsa ist verheiratet. Der Schluß ist bekannt: die berühmte Szene am Flughafen! »Ich schau dir in die Augen, Kleines.« Noch ein kurzer Mord am deutschen Kommandanten, und die üblichen Verdächtigen werden verhaftet. Wie man weiß, der Beginn einer großen Freundschaft zwischen Rick und dem Polizeipräfekten. Daß auch am Schluß die Stadt unsicher bleibt – es herrscht dichter Nebel in der Schlußszene – macht den Ort doppelt rätselhaft. Nicht die malerisch-touristischen Aspekte interessieren, auch nicht der Exotismus – er ist nur beängstigendes Beiwerk –, sondern die privaten Schicksale vor der Kulisse der Geschichte. Jede Stadt ist gleich, würden die Zyniker sagen, einmal ist man in Paris, einmal in New York. Was für Rick zählt, ist der private Freiraum und der Whisky.

Durch die Zusammenfügung von Handlung, Personen und Architektur zum Filmbild entstehen für alle Zeiten festgelegte Kombinationen: Stadt wird zum Bild, aber nicht an sich, sondern immer im Zusammenhang mit einer Geschichte. Der Stadtfilm erklärt die Stadt und verschlüsselt sie gleichzeitig. Er bietet Perspektiven und Sehweisen jeweils aus einer bestimmten menschlichen Lage heraus: Der Verfolgte erlebt die Stadt anders als der Verfolger, der Einsame wieder anders als der Liebende, der Schuljunge wieder anders als der alte Mann.

Der Stadtfilm ist immer ein Möglichkeitsfilm. Der Grad an Pragmatismus oder Utopie, den er mitliefert, entwickelt sich aus seiner Handlung heraus. Heute überwiegen im Film die negativen Stadtvisionen, es zählt nicht mehr die gemütliche Stadtbenutzung wie im französischen Film der dreißiger, vierziger und fünfziger Jahre, bei der sich alle Menschentypen und Lebensentwürfe gleichwertig nebeneinander entfalten durften – so in René Clairs *Unter den Dächern von Paris* (1930), oder in *Die Mausefalle* (1957), auch von René Clair, und bei Marcel Carné und Jacques Tati.

Dort war die Stadt noch die mütterliche Hülle (vor allem Paris), die nachsichtig alles duldete, jedem sein Glas Rotwein und seinen Platz am Tresen gewährte. Vorbei ist es auch mit der Stadtromantik aus Fellinis *Die Müßiggänger* (1953). Höchstens Woody Allen gewährt noch den leicht verklärten Blick auf die Metropole (*Manhattan,* 1979), die Stadtkatastrophen haben sich bei ihm in die Psyche verlagert, und die Stadtbewohner nerven einander mit ihren penetranten Neurosen. Die Gewalt dominiert: *Subway* (1985), *Pulp Fiction* (1994). Auch der Ausblick in die Zukunft ist düster. Die Science-fiction-Städte, die sich aus *Metropolis* entwickelt haben, sind noch gefängnishafter als ihre Vorgänger. Die Überwachungsmechanismen sind total. Ein Entkommen kann es nicht mehr geben: *Blade Runner* (1982), *Batman* (1989).

Diese Entwicklung ist ein Reflex auf die realen Zustände, vor allem in den amerikanischen Städten. Ein ruhiges Leben ist nur noch innerhalb umzäunter und video-gesicherter Ghettos möglich. Jeder, der sich nachts auf die öffentlichen Straßen in Los Angeles zum Beispiel traut, begibt sich in größte Lebensgefahr. Gangs beherrschen die Szene. Jeder Fußgänger und jeder Autofahrer wird zum Freiwild. Ein latenter Bürgerkrieg.

Auch die Fußgängerzonen in den Städten Europas sind zu potentiellen Tatorten geworden. Ihre nächtliche Leere gibt eine Vorahnung der Hölle. Die Zukunft wird noch düsterer werden. Filme vermitteln ein Bild davon.

Dreams turned backwards with leaning gabled houses, crooked walls, corridors and steps as if they had grown naturally.
7. *Der Golem, wie er in die Welt kam*, 1920; directors: Paul Wegener, Carl Boese, architecture: Hans Poelzig.
8, 9. *Faust. Eine deutsche Volkssage*, 1925/26; director: Friedrich Wilhelm Murnau, architecture: Robert Herlth and Walter Röhrig.

Rückwärtsgewandte Träume mit schiefen Giebelhäusern, krummen Wänden, Gängen und Treppen wie naturhaft gewachsen.
7. *Der Golem, wie er in die Welt kam*, 1920; Regie: Paul Wegener, Carl Boese, Architektur: Hans Poelzig.
8, 9. *Faust. Eine deutsche Volkssage*, 1925/26; Regie: Friedrich Wilhelm Murnau, Architektur: Robert Herlth und Walter Röhrig.

10–14. *Metropolis*, 1925/26: director: Fritz Lang, architecture: Otto Hunte, Erich Kettelhut and Karl Vollbrecht.
»It would be possible to suggest today that the only major project in futurist architecture that was ever realized was the model of a city of the future in the Ufa studios in Berlin in which an organ-like steam-siren as tall as a house lets out a summons to work blindly underground, while in the street canyons above columns of flying machines and road vehicles followed their fixed paths through the hierarchically determined order of light and glass.«[3]
»Lang deeply fascinated [on arrival in New York harbour at night]: ›And here just the sight of New York at night would be enough to make this beacon of beauty into the core of a film. It flashes into life, circles in red, blue and the most glowing white, shouts between in green and sinks into black nothing, and is then immediately reborn to experience the play of colours again, streets that are shafts full of light, full of turning, swirling, circling light that seems like an affirmation of joyous life. And above this, high in the sky above the cars and elevated railways, towers of blue and gold, of white and purple appear, called out of the darkness of night by spotlights. Advertisements tower even higher, up to the stars that defeat them in light and splendour, living in ever-new variations.‹«[4]

10–14. *Metropolis*, 1925/26; Regie: Fritz Lang, Architektur: Otto Hunte, Erich Kettelhut und Karl Vollbrecht.
»Man könnte heute behaupten, daß das einzige größere Projekt futuristischer Architektur, das je verwirklicht wurde, jenes Modell einer Zukunftsstadt in den Ufa-Studios in Berlin war, in dem eine ›haushohe‹, orgelartige Dampfsirene zum blinden unterirdischen Arbeitseinsatz ruft, während oben in den Straßenschluchten Flug- und Fahrmaschinenkolonnen ihre festgelegten Wege durch die hierarchisch dynamische Licht- und Glasordnung ziehen.«[3]
»Lang voller Faszination [bei der Ankunft im nächtlichen Hafen von New York]: ›Und dabei müßte allein der Anblick von Neuyork bei Nacht genügen, um dieses Fanal der Schönheit zum Kernpunkt eines Films zu machen. Das blitzt auf, kreist in Rot, Blau und leuchtendem Weiß, schreit in Grün dazwischen und versinkt in schwarzes Nichts, um gleich darauf neugeboren wieder das Spiel der Farben zu erleben, Straßen, die Schächte voll Licht sind, voll drehendem, wirbelndem, kreisendem Licht, das wie ein Bekenntnis zu frohem Leben ist. Und darüber, himmelhoch über den Autos und Hochbahnen, tauchen Türme auf in Blau und Gold, in Weiß und Purpur, von Scheinwerfern aus dem Dunkel der Nacht gerissen. Reklame ragt noch höher, bis zu den Sternen, die diese an Licht und Glanz besiegen, lebend in immer neuer Variation.‹«[4]

The city between romantic transfiguration and science-fiction style demonization.
15. *Blade Runner*, 1982; director: Ridley Scott, architecture: David Snyder (art director), Lawrence G. Pauli (production designer) and Syd Mead (visual futurist).
16. *King Kong*, 1933; director: Merian C. Cooper and Ernest B. Schoedsack, architecture: Carrol Clark and Al Herman.
17. *Sous les toits de Paris*, 1980; direction and screenplay: René Clair, architecture: Lazarc Meerson.
18. *To Catch a Thief*, 1955; director: Alfred Hitchcock, architecture: Hal Pereira and Joseph Macmillan Johnson.

Die Stadt zwischen romantischer Verklärung und sciencefictionhafter Dämonisierung.
15. *Blade Runner,* 1982; Regie: Ridley Scott, Architektur: David Snyder (art director), Lawrence G. Pauli (production designer) und Syd Mead (visual futurist).
16. *King–Kong und die weiße Frau*, 1933; Regie: Merian C. Cooper und Ernest B. Schoedsack, Architektur: Carrol Clark und Al Herman.
17. *Unter den Dächern von Paris* (*Sous les toits de Paris*), 1930; Regie und Drehbuch: René Clair, Architektur: Lazarc Meerson.
18. *Über den Dächern von Nizza*, 1955; Regie: Alfred Hitchcock, Architektur: Hal Pereira und Joseph MacMillan Johnson.

TOW
AWAY
ZONE
NO
STANDING
ANY
TIME

FSK

19. *Manhattan*, 1979; director: Woody Allen, architecture: Mel Bourne.
20, 21. *The Asphalt Jungle*, 1950; director: John Huston, architecture: Cedric Gibbons (art director) and Randall Duell (art director).
22. *Batman*, 1988; director: Tim Burton, architecture: Anton Furst.
23, 24. *M*, 1931; director: Fritz Lang, architecture: Emil Hassler and Karl Vollbrecht.
25. *Dick Tracy*, 1990; producer and director: Warren Beatty, architecture: Harold Michelson (art director) and Richard Sylbert (production design).
26. *The Trial*, 1962; director: Orson Welles, architecture: Jean Mandaroux (art director) and André Labussière (scenic artist).

19. *Manhattan,* 1979; Regie: Woody Allen, Architektur: Mel Bourne.
20, 21. *Asphalt Dschungel,* 1950; Regie: John Huston, Architektur: Cedric Gibbons (art director) und Randall Duell (art director).
22. *Batman,* 1988; Regie: Tim Burton, Architektur: Anton Furst.
23, 24. *M – Eine Stadt sucht einen Mörder,* 1931; Regie: Fritz Lang, Architektur: Emil Hasler und Karl Vollbrecht.
25. *Dick Tracy,* 1990; Produktion und Regie: Warren Beatty, Architektur: Harold Michelson (art director) und Richard Sylbert (production design).
26. *Der Prozeß,* 1962; Regie: Orson Welles, Architektur: Jean Mandaroux (art director) und André Labussière (scenic artist).

19 22
20 23
21 24

Ruined cities

Most urban Utopias in films are negative Utopias, nightmares of war, destruction, violence, repression and captivity. The final step is the extinction of the cities. In *Waterworld* (1995) there are no more countries, the polar ice-caps have melted completely and the whole of the globe is covered with water. All cities are ruins at the bottom of the sea. The last surviving human beings live on primitive artificial atolls and behave like anarchic pirates. A bucket of real earth is traded like gold. There have been films about the ruined city motif throughout the history of the medium. After the end of the Second World War in particular there were enough ruined cities to shoot in. No more glittering neon signs and ceaseless streams of traffic, but a painstakingly cleared path in the city centre, edged with mountains of bricks, and towering over them the battlements of empty façades. A massive cemetery, a hollowed-out range of stone mountains, slowly filling up with life again. Men and women in their wretched clothes go back to the beginning of civilization, happy to have survived – in the mid 20th century: Rossellini's *Germany, Year Zero* (1947/48) or Gerhard Lamprecht's *Irgendwo in Berlin* (1946).

Ruinenstädte

Die meisten Stadtutopien im Film sind negative Utopien. Alpträume von Krieg, Zerstörung, Gewalt, Unterdrückung und Gefangenschaft. Der letzte Schritt besteht in der Auslöschung der Städte. In *Waterworld* (1995) gibt es überhaupt keine Länder mehr, die Eiskappen der Pole sind vollständig abgeschmolzen, das Wasser bedeckt die gesamte Erdkugel. Alle Städte liegen als Ruinen am Grund des Meeres. Die letzten überlebenden Menschen hausen auf primitiven, künstlichen Atollen, ihr Verhalten ist das von anarchistischen Piraten. Ein Eimer voll realer Erde wird gehandelt wie Gold. Im Laufe der Filmgeschichte gibt es immer wieder Filme, die mit dem Motiv der zerstörten Städte arbeiten. Vor allem nach dem Zweiten Weltkrig gab es genügend Ruinenstädte, in denen gedreht werden konnte. Nicht mehr die glitzernden Neonreklamen und das unaufhörliche Strömen des Verkehrs, sondern mitten in der Stadt der mühsam freigelegte Pfad, gesäumt von Bergen aus Ziegeln, überragt von den leeren Fassadenzinnen. Ein gewaltiger Friedhof, ein ausgehöhltes Steingebirge, das sich langsam wieder mit Leben füllt. Die Menschen gehen in armseligen Kleidern zurück zum Anfang der Zivilisation, froh, überlebt zu haben – mitten im 20. Jahrhundert. Rossellinis *Deutschland im Jahre Null* (1947/48) oder Gerhard Lamprechts *Irgendwo in Berlin* (1946).

27. *Germany, Year Zero* (*Germania, Anno Zero*), 1947/48; director: Roberto Rossellini, architecture: Piero Filippone.
28. *Irgendwo in Berlin*, 1946; direction and screenplay: Gerhard Lamprecht, architecture: Otto Erdmann and Wilhelm Vorweg.
29. *A Time to Love and a Time to Die*, 1958; director: Douglas Sirk, architecture: Russell A. Gausman.
30. *Orphée*, 1950; direction and screenplay: Jean Cocteau, architecture: Jean d'Eaubonne.

27. *Deutschland im Jahre Null (Germania, Anno Zero)*, 1947/48; Regie: Roberto Rosselini, Architektur: Piero Filippone.
28. *Irgendwo in Berlin,* 1946; Regie und Buch: Gerhard Lamprecht, Architektur: Otto Erdmann und Wilhem Vorweg.
29. *Zeit zu lieben und Zeit zu sterben*, 1958; Regie: Douglas Sirk, Architektur: Russell A. Gausman.
30. *Orphée,* 1950; Regie und Buch: Jean Cocteau, Architektur: Jean d'Eaubonne.

Streets and roads

Buildings with their offices and rooms tend more towards the private, turning away from the world and hiding their existence, while streets are entirely exterior space, open between the façades, the city's public areas. Buildings are positive forms, streets and roads negative forms. Streets are left-over areas, gaps in the development, necessary for movement. Streets are primarily space for traffic.

In the opening sequence of Joe May's *Asphalt* (1929) we see a road being made. The tar steams, the asphalt is rolled over the ground. The aim is an even, quiet, clean surface. City-dwellers with their elegant clothes and extravagant shoes need this base so that they can move.

All films that begin or are set in streets are looking for the general, anonymity in the mass. The first thing we see in *Asphalt* is the stream of passers-by and traffic. We hear the noise of the city. The story crystallizes out only gradually. Later it withdraws into buildings and rooms. Traffic can be seen constantly streaming past the revolving door of the hotel in *The Last Laugh* (1924) as well. This film draws on the contrast between mass movement outside and isolation within, which then tends to quiet and stillness.

Phil Jutzi's *Berlin-Alexanderplatz* (1931) focuses on a central urban square and the surrounding streets. Franz Biberkopf's drama happens from here outwards. The street as a place for the outcast – with the façades as unwelcoming walls – occurs in numerous films, for example *M* (1931) by Fritz Lang, *The Maltese Falcon* (1941) by John Huston, *The Third Man* (1949) by Carol Reed, *Bicycle Thieves* (1948) by Vittorio de Sica and *The Young and the Damned* (1950) by Luis Buñuel, *Wages of Fear* (1952) by Clouzot, *La Strada* (1955) by Federico Fellini and *Rumble Fish* (1983) by Francis Ford Coppola.

Streets tend to crop up as places of comfortable communication in French and Italian films, e. g. Fellini's *Roma* (1971): a small urban society meets in the evenings to eat spaghetti in a widened street. Trams keep squeaking past in the background. Since the films of the Nouvelle Vague (*Breathless*, 1959, by Godard), the street has also been seen as a place of liberation. This is where you go to escape from your cramped, gloomy home, here you can really live, make contacts and start love affairs.

Scorsese shows the threatening side in *Taxi Driver* (1976/77). New York is seen only from the inside of a taxi. All stories start here. And when the windscreen wiper makes the buildings look blurred, wipes them out and then paints them in again, you realize that the city is the modern landscape, not forests and mountains any more. Cars are suitable architecture, mobile, small, can be used as pleasure steamers or beds, but also as weapons and flight-objects. The buildings outside can be made to fly past. They lose their eternal stone existence.

Anyone who takes to the road will eventually come out into the open. In Godard's *Week End* (1967), driving out into the country is portrayed as an outbreak of mass hysteria, ending in a battlefield of emotions and accidents. The countryside gradually transforms itself into a blazing inferno. In Dennis Hopper's *Easy Rider* (1969) the principal protagonists fall completely under the spell of movement, to the sound of Country and Rock music: their trip takes them from West to East, right across America. They are quite unable to stop, they only have a sense of life when they are on the move. Characters in these films avoid going into or using architecture. At the most they visit a lonely petrol station or motel: *Kings of the Road* (1975) and *Paris, Texas* (1983/84) by Wim Wenders, for example, or *Down by Law* (1986) or *Night on Earth* (1991) by Jim Jarmusch. To a certain extent these road movies are continuations of the Western. Their heroes remain homeless, always driven by insatiable wanderlust.

It was these road movies in particular that were the first to indicate the melancholy beauty of streets and roads, of motorways and highways. Something that is still despised in real architecture and landscape design – the lonely junction in the rain with changing traffic lights, the broad band of asphalt between the trees, the banal, everyday street – was long since discovered here as an expressive, artistic place. It is revalued without many words, in the image. We learn to see the city by looking at film images. A unity that was never planned as such emerges from the many individual building, façade, window, door and shop designs, the design of the pavements, streets and cars.

Straßen

Während die Häuser mit ihren Zimmern und Räumen mehr zum Privaten tendieren, sich von der Welt abwenden, ihr Dasein verbergen, ist die Straße ganz Außenraum, liegt zwischen den Hausfassaden offen, bildet den öffentlichen Bereich der Stadt. Häuser sind Positivformen, Straßen Negativformen. Straßen sind Restflächen, Pausen in der Bebauung, notwendig, um sich fortzubewegen. Straßen sind primär Verkehrsräume.

In der Anfangssequenz von Joe May's *Asphalt* (1929) sieht man, wie eine Straße gebaut wird. Der Teer dampft, der Asphalt wird über die Erde gewalzt. Ziel ist die gleichmäßige, ruhige und saubere Fläche. Diesen Untergrund braucht der Städter mit seinen eleganten Kleidern und seinen extravaganten Schuhen zur Fortbewegung.

Alle auf der Straße beginnenden oder spielenden Filme suchen das Allgemeine, die Anonymität in der Masse. In *Asphalt* sieht man zunächst das Strömen der Passanten und des Verkehrs. Man hört den Lärm der Stadt. Erst allmählich kristallisiert sich die Geschichte heraus. Später zieht sie sich in die Häuser und Räume zurück. Auch in *Der letzte Mann* (1924) sieht man vor der Hoteldrehtür ständig den Verkehr strömen. Diese Filme leben vom Gegensatz zwischen massenhafter Bewegung außen und Vereinzelung innen, die dann zur Ruhe und zum Stillstand tendiert.

In *Berlin-Alexanderplatz* (1931) von Phil Jutzi stehen ein zentraler Stadtplatz und die umliegenden Straßen im Mittelpunkt. Von hier aus ereignet sich das Drama des Franz Biberkopf. Die Straße als Ort des Ausgestoßenseins – mit den Fassaden als abweisenden Wänden – kommt in zahlreichen Filmen vor.

M (1931) etwa von Fritz Lang, *Die Spur des Falken* (1941) von John Huston, *Der dritte Mann* (1949) von Carol Reed, *Die Fahrraddiebe* (1948) von Vittorio de Sica und *Die Vergessenen* (1950) von Luis Buñuel, *Lohn der Angst* (1952) von Clouzot, *La Strada – Das Lied der Straße* (1954) von Federico Fellini und *Rumble Fish* (1982) von Francis Ford Coppola.

Die Straße als Ort der gemütlichen Kommunikation gibt es vor allem in französischen und italienischen Filmen, in Fellinis *Roma* (1971) beispielsweise: Eine kleine Stadtgesellschaft trifft sich abends auf einer erweiterten Straße zum Spaghetti-Essen. Im Hintergrund fährt immer wieder quietschend eine Straßenbahn vorbei. Seit den Filmen der Nouvelle Vague, wie *Außer Atem* (1959) von Godard, gilt die Straße auch als Ort der Befreiung. Hier geht man hin, um den engen und dunklen Wohnungen zu entkommen, hier lebt man sich aus, knüpft Kontakte und beginnt seine Liebesgeschichten.

Die bedrohliche Seite zeigt Scorsese in *Taxi Driver* (1976/77). Man nimmt New York nur noch aus dem Inneren des Taxis wahr. Alle Geschichten haben hier ihren Ursprung. Und wenn der Scheibenwischer die Häuser unscharf erscheinen läßt, auslöscht und wieder hinmalt, erkennt man, daß die Stadt die moderne Landschaft darstellt und nicht mehr der Wald und das Gebirge. Das Auto ist die passende Architektur, mobil, klein, als Vergnügungsdampfer und als Bett verwendbar, aber auch als Waffe und Fluchtobjekt. Die Häuser draußen können zum Vorbeifliegen gebracht werden, sie verlieren ihr ewig steinernes Dasein.

Wer den Straßen folgt, kommt irgendwann ins Freie. In Godards *Weekend* (1967) wird die Fahrt ins Grüne als ausbrechende Massenhysterie geschildert, die in einem Schlachtfeld aus Emotionen und Unfällen endet. Die Landschaft verwandelt sich langsam in ein brennendes Inferno. In Dennis Hoppers *Easy Rider* (1969) verfallen die Hauptdarsteller beim Klang von Country- und Rock-Musik ganz der Bewegung: Ihr Trip führt von West nach Ost, quer durch Amerika. Sie können nicht mehr anhalten, nur in der Fahrbewegung spüren sie das Leben. Die handelnden Personen und Figuren vermeiden das Betreten und Benutzen von Architektur. Allenfalls gehen sie in eine einsame Tankstelle oder in ein Motel: *Im Lauf der Zeit* (1975) und *Paris, Texas* (1983/84) von Wim Wenders beispielsweise, in *Down by Law* (1986) oder *Night on Earth* (1991) von Jim Jarmusch. In gewisser Weise sind diese roadmovies Fortsetzungen der Western. Ihre Helden bleiben heimatlos, immer getrieben von rastlosem Fernweh.

Vor allem die Straßenfilme waren es, die als erste auf die melancholische Schönheit der Stadt- und Landstraßen, der Autobahnen und Highways hingewiesen haben. Was in der realen Architektur und Landschaftsgestaltung immer noch verachtet wird – die einsame Kreuzung im Regen mit blinkenden Ampeln, das breite Asphaltband zwischen den Bäumen, die banale Alltagsstraße –, wurde hier längst als ausdrucksvoller Kunstort entdeckt. Die Umwertung geschieht, ohne viel Worte, im Bild. Beim Betrachten der Filmbilder lernt man die Stadt sehen. Aus den vielen Einzelentwürfen der Häuser, der Fassaden, der Fenster, Türen, Läden, der Bürgersteige, Straßen und Autos entsteht eine so niemals geplante Einheit.

»I have to walk around the streets all time, I have to run, those endless streets ...« says the hunted child-murderer (Peter Lorre) in Fritz Lang's first sound film *M* (1931). Rejected, on the run, in the artificial channel system of the modern metropolis.
31. *Asphalt*, 1929; director: Joe May, architecture: Erich Kettelhut, Robert Herlth and Walter Röhrig.
32. *The Last Laugh*, 1924; director: Friedrich Wilhelm Murnau, architecture: Robert Herlth and Walter Röhrig.
33. *The Woman in the Window*, 1944; director: Fritz Lang, architecture: Duncan Cramer.
34. *M*, 1931; director: Fritz Lang, architecture: Emil Hasler and Karl Vollbrecht.
35. *The Third Man,* 1949; director: Carol Reed, architecture: Vincent Korda.

»Immer muß ich durch Straßen gehen, muß rennen, rennen, endlose Straßen ...«, sagt der gesuchte Kindermörder (Peter Lorre) in Fritz Langs erstem Tonfilm *M – Eine Stadt sucht einen Mörder* (1931). Ausgestoßen, auf der Flucht im künstlichen Kanalsystem der modernen Großstädte.
31. *Asphalt*, 1929; Regie: Joe May, Architektur: Erich Kettelhut, Robert Herlth und Walter Röhrig.
32. *Der letzte Mann,* 1924; Regie: Friedrich Wilhelm Murnau, Architektur: Robert Herlth und Walter Röhrig.
33. *Gefährliche Begegnung,* 1944; Regie: Fritz Lang, Architektur: Duncan Cramer.
34. *M – Eine Stadt sucht einen Mörder*, 1931; Regie: Fritz Lang, Architektur: Emil Hasler und Karl Vollbrecht.
35. *Der Dritte Mann*, 1949; Regie: Carol Reed, Architektur: Vincent Korda.

STYLE MODERNE

The street reflects the psychological condition of the people thrown into the plot. The way is open or closed, the fate is full of possibilities or at an end, without solutions, in front of empty walls, in culs-de-sac.
36, 37. *M*, 1931; director: Fritz Lang, architecture: Emil Hasler and Karl Vollbrecht.
38. *The Young and the Damned* (*Los olvidados*), 1950; director: Luis Buñuel, architecture: Edward Fitzgerald.
39. *Die Straße* (*The Street*), 1923; director: Karl Grune, architecture: Karl Görge and Ludwig Meidner.
40. *Quai des brumes* (*Port of Shadows*), 1938; director: Marcel Carné, architecture: Alexandre Trauner and Paul Bertrand.
41. *Bicycle Thieves* (*Ladri di biciclette*), 1948; director: Vittorio de Sica, architecture: Antonio Traverso.
42. *Zabriskie Point*, 1969; screenplay and direction: Michelangelo Antonioni, architecture: Dean Tavoularis.
43. *Week End*, 1967; screenplay and direction: Jean-Luc Godard.

Die Straße spiegelt die psychischen Zustände der in die Handlung geworfenen Personen. Die Wege sind offen oder verschlossen, die Schicksale voller Möglichkeiten oder am Ende, ohne Lösungen, vor leeren Wänden, in Sackgassen.
36, 37. *M – Eine Stadt sucht einen Mörder,* 1931; Regie: Fritz Lang, Architektur: Emil Hasler und Karl Vollbrecht.
38. *Die Vergessenen* (*Los Olvidados*), 1950; Regie: Luis Buñuel, Architektur: Edward Fitzgerald.
39. *Die Straße,* 1923; Regie: Karl Grune, Architektur: Karl Görge und Ludwig Meidner.
40. *Hafen im Nebel* (*Quai des brumes*), 1938; Regie: Marcel Carné, Architektur: Alexandre Trauner und Paul Bertrand.
41. *Fahrraddiebe* (*Ladri di biciclette*), 1948; Regie: Vittorio de Sica; Architektur: Antonio Traverso.
42. *Zabriskie Point,* 1969; Buch und Regie: Michelangelo Antonioni, Architektur: Dean Tavoularis.
43. *Week End,* 1967; Buch und Regie: Jean-Luc Godard.

36 39
37 40
38 41

And the street as the scene of petit-bourgeois rituals (*Mon oncle*) or anarchistic outbreaks (*A Bout de souffle*).
44. *Mon Oncle*, 1958; screenplay and direction: Jacques Tati, architecture: Henri Schmitt.
45. *Breathless* (*A Bout de souffle)*, 1959; director: Jean-Luc Godard.

Und die Straße als Ort spießiger Rituale (*Mein Onkel*) oder anarchistischer Aufbrüche (*Außer Atem*).
44. *Mein Onkel* (*Mon oncle*), 1958; Buch und Regie: Jacques Tati, Architektur: Henri Schmitt
45. *Außer Atem* (*A Bout de souffle*), 1959; Regie: Jean-Luc Godard.

Again the street is a place for retrospective dreams: a look into another time. Here is the famous »Berlin street« that was used over and over again for the twenties. It was built by Zehetbauer for *The Serpent's Egg* in Gaselgasteig in Munich. Fassbinder later shot his *Berlin-Alexanderplatz* film here. The street has been pulled down now, unfortunately.
46. *The Serpent's Egg* (*Örmens ägg*), 1976; screenplay and direction: Ingmar Bergman, architecture: Rolf Zehetbauer.

Wieder der Straßenraum als Ort des Zurückträumens: Blick in eine andere Zeit. Hier die berühmte, immer wieder benutzte »Berliner Straße«, die für die 20er Jahre in München-Geiselgasteig von Zehetbauer für den Film *Das Schlangenei* gebaut wurde. Später drehte hier Fassbinder seinen Film *Berlin-Alexanderplatz.* Inzwischen ist die Straße leider abgerissen worden.
46. *Das Schlangenei* (*Örmens ägg*), 1976; Buch und Regie: Ingmar Bergmann, Architektur: Rolf Zehetbauer.

The homeless heroes of the road movies.
47, 48. *Kings of the Road*, 1975; screenplay, production and direction: Wim Wenders, architecture: Heidi Lüdi and Bernd Hirskorn.
49. *Down by Law*, 1986; screenplay and direction: Jim Jarmusch, architecture: Roger Knight.

Die heimatlosen Helden der Road-Movies.
47, 48. *Im Lauf der Zeit,* 1975; Buch, Produktion und Regie: Wim Wenders, Architektur: Heidi Lüdi und Bernd Hirskorn.
49. *Down by Law,* 1986; Buch und Regie: Jim Jarmusch, Architektur: Roger Knight.

Houses

The city and the landscape were the great binding elements in the films described so far. It is sometimes enough to tell a story if it is simply linked with a building. The story and psychology of its residents is then closely associated with this building and its rooms. It is as though the building – palace or hut, detached house or motel – tells the story of the film. Of course yet again this can all be traced back to the Expressionist film, *The Cabinet of Dr. Caligari* for example.

Famous buildings in film history have etched themselves into filmgoers' memories: the house in the southern states in *Gone with the Wind* (1939), or the lonely, palace-like house in the middle of the desert in *Giants* (1959), the country house in *Citizen Kane* (1941) and the villa on the cliffs in Hitchcock's *Rebecca* (1940), Charlie Chaplin's wooden house teetering over the cliff in *The Gold Rush* (1924), the factory in *A nous la liberté* (1931) by René Clair, the boarding school buildings in *Zéro de conduite* (1933) by Jean Vigo, *Les Diaboliques* (1954) by Henri Clouzot and in *Young Törless* (1965/66) by Volker Schlöndorf, the picturesque wooden houses in Bodega Bay in Hitchcock's *The Birds* (1963), the castle-like house in the mud-flats in Polanski's *Cul-de-Sac* (1966), the palace in Cocteau's *La Belle et la bête* (1946), the bourgeois modern villa in Tati's *Mon Oncle* (1958), the lonely mountain hotel in Kubrick's *Shining* (1978 bis 1980) and the dream house with the great flight of steps on the roof terrace in Godard's *Le Mépris* (1963).

The more isolated the building is in the landscape, the more the people who live there and visit are exposed to it and feel threatened by it.

The estate in Alfred Hitchcock's *Psycho* (1960) is unforgettable for any filmgoer. Down by the road are the low buildings of the motel that Bates runs, and above them on a hill, accessible up the garden by narrow steps, is a somewhat pathetic, wooden Victorian house pretending to be a little castle, a villa, but somehow radiating the shyness and inhibition of the hero (Anthony Perkins) in architectural terms. It is a long time before viewers of the film penetrate the interior of this building, and when they learn its history and see the mother's mummified corpse they have arrived in the innermost cave of the psyche, in the corridors of aberration and perversion. The interior of the building once more becomes the interior of the hero's ego. The building's façade remains the skin that covers these events.

Psycho also is a good example of the fact that sounds and music are crucial to the effect of a film. Rooms are seldom still in *Psycho*, there is always a rustling, whirring, rumbling, buzzing, a rocking boom. There are symphonic clusters, rhythmic and shrill intensifications. Sometimes operatic, as in Richard Wagner or Richard Strauss, then gentle again, as in Alban Berg. The famous murder scene in the shower cabin would be far less effective without the shrill, cutting notes. Here film becomes a total work of art made up of images, acting, architecture, lighting, camera, direction and music.

Memory has a part to play in many films about buildings. Usually the move in sees the beginning of a new life full of hopes and dreams. Take *Viridiana* (1961) by Luis Buñuel. The characters try to organize their lives and come to terms with their new environment. But often the residents are plagued by fearsome images, and it comes to real nightmares, as in *Halloween* (1978).

In this film, director John Carpenter uses Hitchcock's methods: a typical American detached house idyll is slowly transformed by the power of threat into a highly-charged estate of terror. The plot is simple, the effect powerful. A perverse murderer who comes from this area has escaped from the institution in which he had been confined since his last murder. He drives through the tree-lined residential streets in a stolen car, watching girls coming out of school and making dates for the evening. The viewer never sees all of the murderer, just parts of his body. In the evening, when the children are going from house to house in their Halloween masks and the girls feverishly looking forward to their sexual adventures, the mood intensifies. The murderer slinks across the lawns, flattens himself against wooden walls and looks into the rooms through windows. The camera identifies itself with him, walking, breathing, stumbling. The viewers become voyeurs, villains, murderers, whether they want to or not. As the girls neither know nor suspect anything of the real threat, the awareness of danger and fear first crystallizes in the viewers' heads. Each of them is the third party in the alliance. Finally the murderer gets into the house, and the tension becomes almost intolerable. Then the murder happens, and another one. They each have the effect of an electrical discharge. In the end the murderer is shot by his doctor who has tracked him down. The fact that the dead body disappears after the shot tilts the film into a mythical dimension. The »Black Man« is immortal, and will continue to threaten idylls in future, as they remain vulnerable, susceptible to attack, ultimately illusions based on decent behaviour by everyone.

Perhaps the house is also associated with the summer's erotic experiences (often in Ingmar Bergman's films), with a large or small degree of confusion (Jean Renoir) or everything ends in the final catastrophe and burns down in *The Sacrifice* (1985/86) by Tarkovsky.

In Billy Wilder's *Sunset Boulevard* (1950) the large villa in which the former silent picture star lives has become a private museum under a spell. Only the past counts, Sunset Boulevard's present flows past in the far distance. If a young screenplay writer were not to force his way into the house it would be forgotten for all time. A museum of private myth, full of lies and false dreams. But then life comes back into the rooms again. But the future remains an illusion. At the end the screenplay writer's corpse is floating in the swimming pool.

The house is like a dream bubble in bricks and mortar, romantic and full of promise from the outside, wearing its age with dignity. Inside time seems to have stood still. Anyone who is crossing the threshold steps back fifty years. The house as a vessel for time and the past.

In Alfred Hitchcock's *Shadow of a Doubt* (1943) a typical American small-town house is described. Two storeys, set slightly back from the street – with a strip of lawn in front. A little veranda, stairs inside and out. Everything clean as a new pin and painted white where possible. The rooms are small but not cramped. It is easy to put up a visitor – who later turns out to be a murderer of widows. This brings movement and vigour into everyday life with its rituals like eating, reading the newspaper etc. to a fixed timetable. It is the time when there was not yet a television in every living-room. Few people have curtains; they like to show off their middle-class prosperity. The fact that this visitor brings a deadly threat into this idyll is revealed to the viewer only gradually.

Houses in films – as in life – are places in which to settle, to start a family, bring up children, cook, eat, watch television and sleep. In many recent Hollywood films this house in a green setting is the starting-point for the plot. The story starts and runs its course in the modern living-kitchen in which the family gather in the morning, in Steven Spielberg's *E.T. The Extra-Terrestrial* (1982), for example, or even in *Jaws* (1974). Whether it is a film about love, about education, puberty, an adventure film, a crime film or a horror film emerges only gradually. The house itself remains what it is, the last place of retreat in a hostile world. Threatened in every case by feelings, emotions, real danger or supernatural forces. Dracula or Frankenstein don't have to appear, the Phantom of the Opera or mass murderer Bluebeard: a harmless vacuum-cleaner salesman or an insurance agent is quite enough.

Of course the film is also the place in which architecture can be developed and fantasized further. After the spanish world première of *Metropolis* Buñuel wrote: »From now on and for ever the set designer will be replaced by the architect. The cinema will serve as translator of architecture's boldest dreams.«[5] Opinions may vary about whether these dreams of translation have really become reality.

The fact is that there have continually been films that have not just depicted architecture and buildings as a naturalistic and realistic reproduction of actual urban architecture, but have developed it further by stylization and exaggeration. Here above all we must mention Science Fiction films, for example Kubrick's *2001: A Space Odyssey* (1965–1968) or *Star Wars* (1977–) and *Alien* (1979). The design of these space buildings is intended to move a step ahead of current development and show a world that will perhaps exist in about a thousand years.

The James Bond films have also never allowed their architecture to come to terms with everyday banality. Just think of the places in which the villains live. Sometimes they are underground atomic bunkers, sometimes artificial islands in the sea, or mountain chalets with daringly cantilevered balconies and ingenious window technology. Ken Adams invented and built all these fantastic buildings. Sometimes they give the impression that Frank Lloyd Wright has taken leave of his senses and become possessed by a megalomaniac building craze in a second life. Exaggerated technology might have frightened him as an aberration of his own, but he would have been thrilled by the gigantic runs of rooms and the solid concrete structures.

Often nature is built into the space as well, lumps of rock, palms, water. In the final stages these buildings become utterly evil battlefields. Finally the villain is dealt with, the world saved and the building blown up.

Perhaps these buildings had a certain influence on sixties architecture; think for example of people's fondness for highly cantilevered balconies, large picture windows and their one and only very special view. Technical refinements (automatic doors and lifts etc.) became fashionable as well. You showed who you were and what you had. Architecture as villains presenting themselves! James himself never had a home, he preferred to receive his beauties in hotel rooms.

Häuser

Die Stadt und die Landschaft waren die großen Klammern der bisher beschriebenen Filme. Um eine Geschichte zu erzählen, genügt es manchmal, sie nur mit einem Haus in Verbindung zu bringen. Die Geschichte und die Psychologie der Bewohner ist dann eng mit diesem Haus und seinen Räumen verknüpft. Es ist so, als würde das Haus – Palast oder Hütte, Einfamilienhaus oder Motel – den Film erzählen. Natürlich liegen auch hier die Anfänge im expressionistischen Film, im *Cabinet des Dr. Caligari* (1919) zum Beispiel.

Die berühmten Häuser der Filmgeschichte haben sich in das Gedächtnis aller Filmbesucher der Welt eingegraben: das Südstaatenhaus in *Vom Winde verweht* (1939) oder das einsame, palastartige Haus mitten in der Wüste in *Giganten* (1959), das Schloß aus *Citizen Kane* (1941) und die Villa an der Steilküste in Hitchcocks *Rebekka* (1940), das über die Steilküste gekippte Holzhaus Charlie Chaplins in *Goldrausch* (1924), die Fabrik in *Es lebe die Freiheit* (1931) von René Clair, die Internatsgebäude in *Betragen ungenügend* (1933) von Jean Vigo, in *Die Teuflischen* (1954) von Henri Clouzot und in *Der junge Törless* (1965/66) von Volker Schlöndorf, die malerischen Holzhäuser der Bodega-Bay in Hitchcocks *Die Vögel* (1963), das burgartige Haus im Watt in Polanskis *Wenn Katelbach kommt* (1966), das Schloß in Cocteaus *Die Schöne und das Biest* (1946), die spießig-moderne Villa in Tatis *Mein Onkel* (1958), das einsame Hotel in den Bergen aus Kubricks *Shining* (1978–1980) und das Traumhaus mit großer Freitreppe auf die Dachterrasse in Godards *Die Verachtung* (1963).

Je einsamer das Haus in der Landschaft steht, um so mehr sind die Bewohner und die Besucher ihr ausgesetzt, und um so mehr fühlen sie sich von ihr bedroht.

Unvergeßlich wird jedem Kinobesucher das Anwesen aus *Psycho* (1960) von Alfred Hitchcock sein. Unten an der Straße stehen die niedrigen Häuser des von Bates betriebenen Motels und oben auf einem Hügel, über eine schmale Gartentreppe erreichbar, das etwas armselige, hölzerne, viktorianische Haus, das vorgibt, ein kleines Schloß zu sein, eine Villa, aber irgendwie das Schüchtern-Verklemmte des Helden (Anthony Perkins) architektonisch ausstrahlt. Erst spät dringt der Filmbetrachter ins Innere dieses Hauses ein, und als er seine Geschichte erfährt und die mumifizierte Leiche der Mutter sieht, ist er angekommen in der innersten Höhle der Psyche, in den Gängen der Verirrung und Perversion. Hausinnenraum wird wieder zum Ichinnenraum des Helden. Hausfassade bleibt die verhüllende Haut um dieses Geschehen.

Psycho ist auch ein gutes Beispiel dafür, daß Geräusche und Musik entscheidend für die Wirkung eines Films sind. In *Psycho* gibt es nur selten stille Räume, immer hört man ein Schwirren, Surren, Brummeln, Sirren, schaukelndes Dröhnen. Es gibt symphonische Cluster, rhythmische und schrille Steigerungen. Opernhaft manchmal, wie bei Richard Wagner oder Richard Strauss, dann wieder sanft wie bei Alban Berg. Die berühmte Mordszene in der Duschzelle wäre ohne die schrillen, spitzen Töne weit weniger wirkungsvoll. Film wird hier zum Gesamtkunstwerk aus Bildern, Schauspielkunst, Architektur, Licht, Kamera, Regie und Musik.

In vielen Haus-Filmen spielen Erinnerungen eine Rolle. Meist beginnt mit dem Einzug ein neues Leben voller Hoffnungen und Träume, *Viridiana* (1961) etwa von Luis Buñuel. Man versucht, sein Leben einzurichten, sich mit der neuen Umgebung zu arrangieren. Aber oft überfallen Angstbilder die Bewohner, es kommt zu wahren Alpträumen wie in *Halloween* (1978).

In diesem Film greift der Regisseur John Carpenter die Methoden Hitchcocks auf: Eine typische amerikanische Einfamilienhausidylle wird langsam durch Bedrohung in eine mit Hochspannung aufgeladene Angstsiedlung verwandelt. Der Plot ist einfach, die Wirkung stark. Aus einer Anstalt ist ein perverser Mörder, der aus dieser Gegend stammt, ausgebrochen. Er fährt mit einem gestohlenen Wagen durch die von großen Bäumen gesäumten Wohnstraßen und beobachtet Mädchen, die aus der Schule kommen und sich für den Abend verabreden. Der Zuschauer sieht den Mörder nie ganz, immer nur Teile seines Körpers. Am Abend, als die Kinder mit ihren Halloween-Masken von Haus zu Haus ziehen und die Mädchen ihren erotischen Abenteuern entgegenfiebern, verdichtet sich die Stimmung. Der Mörder schleicht über die Wiesen, drückt sich an Holzwänden entlang und blickt in die Fenster der Zimmer. Die Kamera identifiziert sich mit ihm, sie geht, atmet, stolpert. Der Zuschauer wird zum Voyeur, zum Bösewicht, zum Mörder, ob er will oder nicht. Da die Mädchen von der realen Bedrohung nichts wissen oder sie auch nur erahnen, vollendet sich das Bewußtsein von Gefahr und Angst erst im Kopf des Zuschauers. Er ist der Dritte im Bunde. Schließlich dringt der Mörder in das Haus ein, die Spannung steigert sich bis ins fast Unerträgliche. Dann geschieht der Mord, dann ein weiterer. Die Taten wirken wie elektrische Entladungen. Am Ende wird der Mörder von seinem Arzt erschossen, der ihn verfolgt hat. Daß der tote Körper nach dem Schuß verschwunden ist, läßt den Film in eine mythische Dimension umkippen: Der »Schwarze Mann« ist unsterblich, er wird in Zukunft auch weiterhin Idyllen bedrohen, denn diese bleiben verletzbar, angreifbar, Illusionen letztlich, die auf dem anständigen Verhalten aller beruhen.

Vielleicht ist das Haus auch mit den erotischen Erlebnissen eines Sommers verknüpft (oft bei Ingmar Bergman), mit einer kleinen oder großen Verwirrung (bei Jean Renoir), oder es endet in der finalen Katastrophe und brennt ab, wie in dem Film *Opfer* (1985/86) von Tarkowski.

In *Boulevard der Dämmerung* (1950) von Billy Wilder ist die große Villa, in der eine ehemalige Stummfilmdiva wohnt, zu einem verwunschenen Privatmuseum geworden. Nur noch die Vergangenheit zählt, die Gegenwart des Sunset Boulevard strömt in weiter Ferne vorbei. Wenn nicht eines Tages dieser junge Drehbuchautor in das Haus eingedrungen wäre, hätte man es für alle Zeiten vergessen. Ein privatmythologisches Mausoleum, voller Lügen und falscher Träume. Doch dann kommt noch einmal Leben in die Räume. Aber die Zukunft bleibt eine Illusion. Am Ende treibt der Drehbuchautor als Leiche im Swimmingpool.

Das Haus ist wie eine gebaute Traumblase, von außen romantisch und voller Versprechungen, sein Alter mit Würde tragend. Innen scheint die Zeit stehengeblieben zu sein. Wer die Türschwelle überschreitet, tritt fünfzig Jahre zurück. Das Haus als Gefäß von Zeit und Vergangenheit.

In *Im Schatten des Zweifels* (1943) von Alfred Hitchcock wird ein typisches amerikanisches Kleinstadthaus beschrieben. Zweistöckig, leicht von der Straße zurückversetzt – mit Grünstreifen davor. Eine kleine Veranda, Innen- und Außentreppe. Alles blitzsauber und weiß gestrichen, wo nur möglich. Die Räume sind klein, aber nicht eng. Man kann einen Besucher – der sich später als Witwenmörder entpuppt – leicht aufnehmen. Das bringt Bewegung und Belebung in den Alltag mit seinen nach festem Zeitplan ablaufenden Ritualen wie Essen, Zeitunglesen usw. Es ist die Zeit, in der noch nicht in jedem Wohnzimmer ein Fernseher stand. Man hat kaum Vorhänge, zeigt sein bürgerliches Wohlverhalten gern. Daß sich mit dem Besucher langsam tödliche Bedrohung in die Idylle einschleicht, offenbart sich dem Betrachter erst allmählich.

Häuser im Film sind – wie im Leben – Orte, um sich niederzulassen, eine Familie zu gründen, Kinder großzuziehen, zu kochen, zu essen, fernzusehen und zu schlafen. In vielen Hollywood-Filmen der letzten Jahre ist dieses Haus im Grünen der Ausgangspunkt der Handlung. Aus der modernen Wohnküche heraus, in der sich die Familie morgens versammelt, nimmt die Geschichte ihren Anfang und ihren Verlauf, bei Steven Spielberg in *E.T. – Der Außerirdische* (1982) oder auch schon im *Weißen Hai* (1974). Ob es ein Liebesfilm wird, ein Erziehungsfilm, ein Pubertätsfilm, ein Abenteuerfilm, ein Kriminalfilm oder ein Horrorfilm, das erfährt man erst nach und nach. Das Haus selbst bleibt das, was es ist, letzter Rückzugsort in einer feindlichen Welt, in jedem Fall bedroht, durch Gefühle, Emotionen, reale Gefahren oder außerirdische Kräfte. Es muß ja nicht gleich Dracula oder Frankenstein auftauchen, das Phantom aus der Oper oder der Massenmörder Blaubart, es genügt bereits ein harmloser Staubsaugervertreter oder der Agent einer Versicherungsfirma.

Natürlich ist der Film auch der Ort, die Architektur der Häuser weiterzudenken, fortzuphantasieren. Nach der spanischen Uraufführung von *Metropolis* schrieb Buñuel: »An die Stelle des Bühnenbildners tritt von nun an und für immer der Architekt. Das Kino wird den kühnsten Träumen der Architektur als treuer Übersetzer dienen.«[5] Ob diese Übersetzungsträume wirklich geleistet worden sind, darüber kann man verschiedener Meinung sein.

Tatsache ist, daß es immer wieder Filme gegeben hat, die Architektur und Häuser nicht nur als naturalistisch-realistische Wiedergabe der tatsächlichen Architektur der Städte abgebildet, sondern durch Stilisierung und Übertreibung weiterentworfen haben. Hier muß vor allem der Science-fiction-Film erwähnt werden, etwa Kubricks *2001: Odyssee im Weltall* (1965–1968) oder *Krieg der Sterne* (1977–) und *Alien – Das unheimliche Wesen aus einer fremden Welt* (1979). Das Design dieser Weltall-Häuser, innen und außen, will der Entwicklung vorausgreifen und eine Welt zeigen, die es vielleicht in tausend Jahren einmal geben wird.

Auch die James-Bond-Filme haben sich in ihrer Architektur nie mit der banalen Alltagswelt abgefunden. Denken wir nur an die Wohnhäuser der Bösewichter. Mal sind es unterirdische Atombunker, mal künstliche Inseln im Meer, mal Châlets im Gebirge mit gewagt auskragenden

Balkonen und ausgeklügelter Fenstertechnik. Ken Adams hat all diese fantastischen Gebäude erfunden und gebaut. Manchmal hat man das Gefühl, Frank Llyod Wright sei außer sich geraten und in einem zweiten Leben von einer größenwahnsinnigen Baumanie erfaßt worden. Die übertriebene Technik hätte ihn vielleicht als eine eigene Verirrung erschreckt, über die riesigen Raumfluchten jedoch und die soliden Betonkonstruktionen wäre er erfreut gewesen.

Oft ist auch Natur mit in den Raum eingebaut, Felsbrocken, Palmen, Wasser. Im Countdown werden diese Gebäude zu Orten übelster Schlachten. Am Ende ist der Bösewicht erledigt, die Welt gerettet und das Gebäude in die Luft gesprengt.

Vielleicht haben diese Räume eine gewisse Wirkung auf die Architektur der sechziger Jahre ausgeübt, denkt man beispielsweise an die Vorliebe für weit auskragende Balkone, die großen Ausblickfenster und die Sehnsucht nach dem besonderen Blick. Auch die technischen Finessen (automatische Türen und Aufzüge usw.) kamen in Mode. Man zeigte, was man hat und wer man ist. Architektur als Selbstdarstellung der Bösewichter! James selbst hat nie eine Wohnung, er pflegt seine Schönen in Hotelzimmern zu empfangen.

Houses of life, of love, of hope, of happiness, houses of fear, of extortion, of despair, houses of psychological confusion, of illness and of death.
50. *Rebecca,* 1940; director: Alfred Hitchcock, architecture: Lyle Wheeler.
51. *Gone with the Wind*, 1939; director: Victor Fleming, architecture: Lyle Wheeler (art director) and William Cameron Menzies (production designer).

Häuser des Lebens, der Liebe, der Hoffnung, des Glücks, Häuser der Angst, der Erpressung, der Verzweiflung, Häuser der psychischen Verwirrung, der Krankheit und des Todes.
50. *Rebekka,* 1940; Regie: Alfred Hitchcock; Architektur: Lyle Wheeler.
51. *Vom Winde verweht*, 1939; Regie: Victor Fleming, Architektur: Lyle Wheeler (art direktor) und William Cameron Menzies (production designer).

52. *Les Diaboliques*, 1954; director: Henri-Georges Clouzot, architecture: Léon Barsacq.
53. *A nous la liberté*, 1931; direction and screenplay: René Clair, architecture: Lazare Meerson.
54, 55. *Psycho*, 1960; director: Alfred Hitchcock, architecture: Joseph Hurley, Robert Clatworthy and George Milo.

52. *Die Teuflischen* (*Les Diaboliques*), 1954; Regie: Henri-Georges Clouzot, Architektur: Léon Barsacq.
53. *Es lebe die Freiheit* (*A nous la liberté*), 1931; Regie und Buch: René Clair, Architektur: Lazare Meerson.
54, 55. *Psycho,* 1960; Regie: Alfred Hitchcock, Architektur: Joseph Hurley, Robert Clatworthy und George Milo.

Film architecture is never a silent shell, standing there indifferently, every façade, every building is involved and has something to say. Door and window are narrative elements, darkness and brightness, light and shade have a dramaturgic function.
56. *Viridiana*, 1961; screenplay and direction: Luis Buñuel, architecture: Francisco Canet.
57. *Young Törless / Les desarrois de l'élève Toerless*, 1965/66; screenplay and direction: Volker Schlöndorff, architecture: Marleen Pacha.

Filmarchitektur ist nie teilnahmslos dastehende schweigende Hülle, jede Fassade, jedes Haus mischt sich ein, spricht mit. Tor und Fenster sind Elemente der Erzählung. Dunkelheiten und Helligkeiten, Licht und Schatten haben eine dramaturgische Funktion.
56. *Viridiana,* 1961; Buch und Regie: Luis Buñuel, Architektur: Francisco Canet.
57. *Der junge Törless / Les desarrois de l'élève Toerless*, 1965/66; Buch und Regie: Volker Schlöndorff, Architektur: Marleen Pacha.

Houses in the fog, erotically crackling houses, glowing houses, burning houses. Film architecture can make the invisible visible, can translate function into emotion and release things that have been suppressed.
58. *The Exorcist*, 1973; director: William Friedkin, architecture: Bill Malley.
59. *Viridiana*, 1961; screenplay and direction: Luis Buñuel, architecture: Francisco Canet.
60, 61. *The Sacrifice* (*Offret / Le Sacrifice*), 1985/1986; director: Andrej Tarkovskij, architecture: Anna Asp.

Eingenebelte Häuser, erotisch knisternde Häuser, glühende Häuser, brennende Häuser. Filmarchitektur kann das Unsichtbare sichtbar machen, kann die Funktion zur Emotion umdeuten und das Verdrängte aufbrechen lassen.
58. *Der Exorzist*, 1973; Regie: William Friedkin: Architektur: Bill Malley.
59. *Viridiana,* 1961; Buch und Regie: Luis Buñuel, Architektur: Francisco Canet.
60, 61. *Opfer* (*Offret / Le sacrifice*), 1979; Regie: Andrej Tarkowskij, Architektur: Anna Asp.

Views of the houses of the subconscious, the dream, the future, above ground, under the ground, in space. Film architecture as an experimental laboratory.
62. *2001: A Space Odyssey*, 1965–1968; producer and director: Stanley Kubrick, architecture: John Hoesli (art director), Tony Masters, Harry Lange and Ernest Archer (production design).
63. *James Bond 007 –You only Live Twice,* 1966; director: Lewis Gilbert, architecture: Ken Adam.
64. *E. T. The Extra-Terrestrial*, 1982; producer and director: Steven Spielberg, architecture: James D. Bissell.

Blicke auf die Häuser des Unterbewußtseins, des Traums, der Zukunft, über der Erde, unter der Erde, im Weltall. Filmarchitektur als Versuchslabor.
62. *2001: Odyssee im Weltraum,* 1965–1968; Produktion und Regie: Stanley Kubrick, Architektur: John Hoesli (art director), Tony Masters, Harry Lange und Ernest Archer (production design).
63. *James Bond 007– Man lebt nur zweimal*, 1966; Regie: Lewis Gilbert, Architektur: Ken Adam.
64. *E. T.– Der Außerirdische,* 1982; Produktion und Regie: Steven Spielberg, Architektur: James D. Bissell.

Rooms

Rooms are always part of a building, their interior, their hollow space. There are films that are more interested in these rooms than in the exterior of the building. We often do not see the whole building, or sometimes in reduced form, like a model.

Rooms also provide character for the heroes of films, reflect their mood, their social status, their rise and fall. There are shabby rooms, middle-class dwellings, trendy lofts, neutral offices, lavish rooms in palaces, pompous ostentatious living-rooms, bedrooms with enormous windows (with a view of a Paris backyard or Central Park in New York). Everyone who lives in these rooms has arrived here, and hides, contrasting with the roomless heroes of Westerns or road movies.

Gloomy rooms without light can scarcely be used in films. Their visibility is the deciding factor, and light decides about this. It gets in through little holes in the wall or ceiling, through glazed sections of the wall, through skylights, or it shines visibly from artificial light sources – candles, electric light-bulbs, lamps, neon tubes or chandeliers. There is warm light, cold light, pale light or harsh light with hard-edged shadows, even illumination in an office or hospital ward, the neutral brightness of a library, comfortable light in a pub, sophisticated light in a flat, sparse light in a hotel room etc. Rooms illuminated only by candles in Kubrick's *Barry Lyndon* (1973–1975), Alekan's magic lighting in Cocteau's films.

The actors' bodies are placed in the room, their faces are evenly lit, or there may be just a narrow strip of light on their forehead. Films set in rooms are ideal for studying the effects of various lighting options. Atmosphere in a room is primarily the atmosphere of its light.

Many film rooms have etched themselves so deeply in our memories that we could swear we have seen them: the bedroom with a cow on the bed in Luis Buñuel's *L'âge d'or* (1930), the fortress cells in Jean Renoir's *La grande illusion* (1937), Rick's café in *Casablanca* (1942), the hotel hall in Lubitsch's *Ninotchka* (1939), Humphrey Bogart's shabby detective's office in *The Big Sleep* (1946), the garage in Cocteau's *Orphée* (1950), in which Jean Marais makes contact with the other world by means of the car's radio, the elegant living-rooms in Cukor's *The Women* (1939), Jean Harlow's villa in *Bombshell* (1933) after she has achieved film fame, the ship's cabin in Helmut Käutner's *Unter den Brücken* (1946), the brothel room in Luis Buñuel's *Belle de jour* (1967), the comfortable sitting-room in the wooden house in Bodega Bay in which a swarm of threatening birds suddenly bursts out of the fireplace in Alfred Hitchcock's *The Birds* (1963), Tony Curtis's and Jack Lemon's hotel-room and bathroom in *Some Like It Hot* (1959) by Billy Wilder, or rooms in films by Josef von Sternberg.

In *Shanghai-Express* (1932) he restricts the room to alleys, passages and corridors. Light falls exclusively from above, so that the characters move as though in a trench system. Beams lying diagonally across the paths throw long, oblique shadows over the irregularly plastered walls, emphasizing the prison-like character of the architecture. No-one has made hollow space more visible than Sternberg. His design resources were movement, light and shade, sometimes smoke, mist and sounds as well. At the beginning of *The Blue Angel* the hooting of a large ship is heard in the distance. This indicates distance as space and opportunity. But because the protagonists carry confinement in their heads they do not hear the hooting and torment each other to death.

All Sternberg's characters move along walls or occupy their narrow spaces close to these walls. They avoid open, empty spaces. Space is always an emotional prison here; it offers protection, but restricts or scarcely permits freedom of movement. Sternberg equates stepping out into open space with a decision in favour of danger, of latent anarchy, but also of total love. At the end of *Morocco*, for instance, when Marlene Dietrich goes through the town gate into the desert, takes off her shoes and follows the soldiers, including her lover.

John Huston too, brillantly describes rooms, e. g. the shabby hotel hall in *Key Largo* (1948). This wooden hotel hall is somewhere at the end of the world, represented here by the southernmost tip of Florida. A bunch of men and of women hoping for a big deal (with forged money, as it later emerges). They have all seen better days. The fascinating thing about this room is its atmosphere and the description of an increasing threat. First the stifling heat. The slowly turning ceiling-fan. The heat is mentioned, each of the characters suffers from it in a different way. Thirst, constant drinking. Then the threat emanating from the gangsters, harmless at first, then becoming increasingly serious, finally involving pistols and physical violence. They are not even afraid to kill (a policeman who gets in). But the actual climax is an approaching hurricane. The danger is described in words at first, then the wind starts to get up, the shutters rattle, they are closed one after the other. Then the storm breaks, the wind whistles through the cracks, the glasses wobble, a window breaks – and at the same time we see how the people in the room react. The gangster boss (Robinson) is the most afraid.

This piece of film narrative is one of the finest examples in film history of the atmosphere of a room, imagined and real threat and personal mood fusing together.

There are characters who are scarcely aware of the space they are in, where others suffer in certain spaces. It is important how well the person knows the space in which he is. Whether he is going into it for the first time (strange shop, strange station, strange home), or for the tenth. Our own home is of course the most familiar. Here every corner is internalized. We could probably find our way around with our eyes shut. There is something studied, ritualistic, hackneyed about all our movements. There are no curious looks any more, just short glances, checking. Every detail is memorable. We remember every detail – just as we left it. But the filmgoer is seeing the film for the first time. This leads to a difference in information levels that can be covered by the length of time for which the camera lingers. Or the film chooses rooms that are unknown to both the actors and the viewers. Hotels are most suitable for this. There are countless films set in hotels. It is always unfamiliar anonymity that is described for the film viewer as the character arrives. Every arrival has to define himself anew, his character is not fixed by a home in which he has lived for a long time.

Ingmar Bergman picks up all these motifs in *The Silence* (1963). Two women (sisters) and a little boy (son of one of the women) arrive by train in a strange town in a strange country. They do not understand the language. We see life outside in fragments, lively activity, but also military movements, tanks are being transported, and later a tank will appear outside the window in the middle of the night. They will not find out whether there is a real threat or it is just harmless manœuvres. The hotel too is shown only in fragments, and never from outside.

No-one seems to live here except for a troupe of midgets who are appearing at the local variety theatre. Although the women settle in quickly in domestic terms, the alien anonymity of the place is a persisting theme. To a certain extent it is again an outward manifestation of the emotional state of the women and the child. The child in particular feels that the corridors and passageways are a frightening labyrinth, with the floor waiter as a black spider. This waiter has to spend his days in a tiny room waiting for the guests to ring; he once more embodies the hotel, focuses the danger that it contains, but also all its protective humanity. We can believe that there is yearning in his touch, but also the abyss of pederasty.

In the hotel room itself there is war between the women, a love-hate tension field. *The Silence* is a film of looks, long fixed looks into space (the sick female translator), lustful looks from the nymphomaniac (the mother), the little boy's inquisitive and anxious gaze. Then looks exchanged between the characters, woman to woman, woman to man, child to woman, the woman looking out of the window, the child looking out into the corridor and at the old waiter. The other person is a reflection that is questioned and not understood, the room remains the silent casing, the hotel the rented covering, the protective space into which they crawl. The sexual tensions between the characters keep breaking through as if from a different, subliminal world. They are archaic forces that attack body and mind in an uncontrolled fashion, poisonous, full of perverse depths. They are compulsive desires, determining how the characters lie, walk, stand and look. Without these forces life might be tolerable, the hotel might be a pleasant place, but as things are it increasingly transforms itself into a place of passion, shortly before the end, before the crucifixion. There is no understanding, words are inadequate – they lie – the room becomes a trap, all they can do in these beds is get drunk, go even more deeply into themselves or look for quick sex.

Räume

Räume sind immer Teil eines Hauses, ihre Innenseite, ihr Hohlraum. Es gibt viele Filme im Verlauf der Filmgeschichte, die sich mehr für diese Räume interessieren als für die Hausaußenseite. Man sieht die Häuser oft nie ganz oder manchmal nur in modellhafter Verkleinerung.

Auch Räume charakterisieren die Helden der Filme, geben ihre Stimmung wieder, ihren gesellschaftlichen Stand, ihren Aufstieg und ihren Abstieg. Es gibt schäbige Zimmer, bürgerliche Wohnungen, modische Lofts, sachliche Büros, üppige Schloßräume, pompöse Angeberwohnräume, Schlafzimmer mit riesigen Fenstern (Blick auf einen Pariser Hinterhof oder auf den Centralpark in New York). Jeder Bewohner eines Raums ist angekommen, versteckt sich hier.

Er steht im Gegensatz zu dem raumlosen Helden etwa der Western-Filme oder der road movies.

Dunkle, lichtlose Räume sind im Film kaum verwendbar. Entscheidend ist ihre Sichtbarkeit. Und über diese entscheidet das Licht. Es fällt durch kleine Löcher in der Wand oder in der Decke, durch verglaste Wandteile, durch Oberlichtdächer, oder es strahlt sichtbar aus künstlichen Lichtquellen – Kerzen, elektrischen Birnen, Lampen, Neonröhren oder Kronleuchtern. Es gibt warmes Licht, kaltes Licht, fahles Licht oder grelles Licht mit Schlagschatten. Gleichmäßige Helligkeit eines Büroraums oder eines Krankenhausraums, sachliche Helligkeit einer Bibliothek, gemütliches Licht einer Kneipe, raffiniertes Licht einer Wohnung, sparsames Licht eines Hotelzimmers usw. Nur von Kerzen beleuchtete Räume in Kubricks *Barry Lyndon* (1973 bis 1975). Alekans Lichtzaubereien in den Filmen Cocteaus.

Im Raum stehen die Körper der Schauspieler, ihre Gesichter sind gleichmäßig ausgeleuchtet, oder nur ein schmaler Lichtstreifen fällt über ihre Stirn. Filme, die in Räumen spielen, sind ideale Studienobjekte für die Wirkungen der verschiedenen Beleuchtungsmöglichkeiten. Raumatmosphäre ist primär Lichtatmosphäre.

Manche Filmräume haben sich so tief ins Gedächtnis eingegraben, daß man schwören könnte, sie in Wirklichkeit gesehen zu haben: Das Schlafzimmer mit einer Kuh auf dem Bett in *Das goldene Zeitalter* (1930) von Luis Buñuel, die Festungshafträume in *Die große Illusion* (1937) von Jean Renoir, Ricks Café in *Casablanca* (1942), die Hotelhalle in Lubitschs *Ninotschka* (1939), das schäbige Detektivbüro von Humphrey Bogart in *Tote schlafen fest* (1946), die Garage in Cocteaus *Orphée* (1950), in der Jean Marais Kontakt über das Autoradio mit dem Jenseits aufnimmt, die eleganten Wohnräume in Cukors *Frauen* (1939), die Villa von Jean Harlow in *Die Sexbombe* (1933), nachdem sie zu Filmruhm aufgestiegen ist, der Schiffsraum in Helmut Käutners *Unter den Brücken* (1946), der Bordellraum in *Schöne des Tages* (1967) von Luis Buñuel, der gemütliche Wohnzimmerraum im Holzhaus an der Bodega-Bay, in den plötzlich durch den Kamin ein Schwarm bedrohlicher Vögel hereinbricht in *Die Vögel* (1963) von Alfred Hitchcock, das Hotel- und Badezimmer von Tony Curtis und Jack Lemon in *Manche mögen's heiß* (1959) von Billy Wilder oder die Räume in den Filmen Josef von Sternbergs.

In *Shanghai-Express* (1932) verengt er den Raum zu Gassen, Gängen und Korridoren. Das Licht fällt ausschließlich von oben ein, so daß sich die Figuren bewegen wie in einem Grabensystem. Quer über den Wegen liegende Balken werfen schräge, langgezogene Schatten über die unregelmäßig verputzten Wände, wodurch der Gefängnischarakter der Architektur betont wird. Keiner hat den Hohlraum so sichtbar gemacht wie Sternberg. Bewegung, Licht und Schatten, manchmal auch Rauch, Nebel und Geräusche waren seine Gestaltungsmittel. Am Anfang von *Der Blaue Engel* hört man in der Ferne das Tuten eines großen Schiffes. Damit wird die Ferne als Raum und Möglichkeit angedeutet. Aber weil die handelnden Figuren die Enge in ihrem Kopf tragen, hören sie das Tuten nicht und quälen einander zu Tode.

Alle Figuren bei Sternberg bewegen sich an den Wänden entlang oder halten sich in ihren engen Räumen in der Nähe dieser Wände auf. Den offenen, leeren Raum meiden sie. Raum ist hier immer emotionales Gefängnis, das zwar Schutz bietet, aber die Bewegungsfreiheit einschränkt oder kaum zuläßt. Das Betreten des offenen Raums setzt Sternberg gleich mit der Entscheidung zur Gefahr, zur latenten Anarchie, aber auch zur totalen Emotion der Liebe. Etwa am Schluß von *Marokko*, wenn Marlene Dietrich durch das Stadttor in die Wüste hinaustritt, ihre Schuhe auszieht und den Soldaten folgt, unter denen ihr Geliebter ist.

Auch John Huston ist ein Meister der Raumbeschreibung, die schäbige Hotelhalle in *Hafen des Lasters / Gangster vor Key Largo* (1948) zum Beispiel. Diese hölzerne Hotelhalle steht irgendwo am Ende der Welt, das hier von der Südspitze Floridas dargestellt wird. Mehrere Männer und eine Frau, die auf das große Geschäft hoffen (mit Falschgeld, wie sich später herausstellt). Alle haben bessere Zeiten gesehen. Das Faszinierende an diesem Raum ist seine Atmosphäre und die Beschreibung einer sich steigernden Bedrohung. Erst die brütende Hitze. Der immer langsam kreisende Deckenventilator. Das Erwähnen der Hitze, jede Person leidet anders unter ihr. Durst, ständiges Trinken. Dann die Bedrohung, die von den Gangstern ausgeht, harmlos zuerst, dann immer ernster werdend, schließlich mit Pistolen und körperlicher Gewalt. Selbst vor Mord (an einem eindringenden Polizisten) wird nicht zurückgeschreckt. Der eigentliche Höhepunkt jedoch ist das Heraufziehen eines Hurricans. Die Gefahr wird zunächst verbal beschrieben, dann kommt tatsächlich Wind auf, die Läden klappern, sie werden nacheinander geschlossen. Schließlich bricht das Unwetter los, der Wind pfeift durch die Ritzen, die Gläser wackeln, ein Fenster bricht – gleichzeitig werden die Reaktionen der Personen geschildert, die sich im Raum befinden. Am meisten Angst hat der Obergangster (Robinson).

Diese Filmschilderung ist eines der schönsten Beispiele der Filmgeschichte für die langsame Ineinanderverschmelzung von Raumstimmung, eingebildeter und realer Bedrohung und Personenstimmung.

Es gibt Figuren, die den Raum, in dem sie sich befinden, überhaupt nicht wahrnehmen, andere Figuren wiederum leiden an bestimmten Räumen. Wichtig ist, wie gut eine Person den Raum kennt, in dem sie sich aufhält. Betritt man ihn zum ersten Mal (fremdes Geschäft, frem der Bahnhof, fremde Wohnung), oder betritt man ihn bereits zum zehnten Mal. Die eigene Wohnung kennt man natürlich am besten. Hier ist jeder Winkel verinnerlicht. Man würde sich darin vielleicht auch mit geschlossenen Augen zurechtfinden. Alle Bewegungen haben etwas Eingespieltes, Rituelles, Abgedroschenes. Es gibt keine neugierigen Blicke mehr, höchstens kurze überprüfende. Man erinnert sich an jedes Detail – wie man es zurückgelassen hat. Der Filmbetrachter sieht den Raum dagegen zum ersten Mal. Es kommt zu einer Differenz an Information, die durch das längere Verweilen der Kamera überspielt werden kann. Oder man wählt im Film Räume, die weder Schauspieler noch Betrachter kennen. Hier eignet sich das Hotel am besten. Es gibt unzählige Filme, die in Hotels spielen. Stets ist es die Anonymität, die mit dem Ankommenden für den Filmbetrachter beschrieben wird. Jeder Ankommende muß sich neu definieren, ist nicht durch eine Wohnung, in der er bereits seit langem lebt, im Charakter festgelegt.

In *Das Schweigen* (1963) nimmt Ingmar Bergman alle diese Motive auf. Mit dem Zug kommen zwei Frauen (Schwestern) und ein kleiner Junge (Sohn der einen Frau) in einer fremden Stadt, in einem fremden Land an. Man versteht die Sprache nicht. In Fragmenten sieht man das Leben draußen, reges Treiben, aber auch militärische Aktivitäten, Panzer werden transportiert, später wird ein Panzer mitten in der Nacht vor dem Fenster auftauchen. Man wird nicht erfahren, ob es sich um eine reale Bedrohung oder nur ein harmloses Manöver handelt. Das Hotel selbst sieht man auch nur in Fragmenten, nie von außen.

Bis auf eine Gruppe von Liliputanern, die im örtlichen Varieté auftreten, scheint hier niemand zu wohnen. Obwohl sich die Frauen schnell häuslich einrichten, bleibt die fremde Anonymität des Ortes ein bestimmendes Thema. Sie ist in gewisser Weise wieder der nach außen gekehrte Gemütszustand der Frauen und auch des Kindes. Vor allem das Kind erlebt die Gänge und Flure als beängstigendes Labyrinth, mit dem Etagenkellner als schwarzer Spinne. Er, der in einer kleinen Kammer seine Tage verbringen muß und auf das Klingeln der Gäste wartet, verkörpert das Hotel noch einmal, bündelt dessen Gefahr und dessen beschützende Menschlichkeit. Man traut seiner Berührung Sehnsucht zu, aber auch den Abgrund der Päderastie.

Im Hotelzimmer selbst herrscht Krieg zwischen den Frauen, ein Spannungsfeld aus Haßliebe. *Das Schweigen* ist ein Film der Blicke, lange starre Blicke vor sich hin (die kranke Übersetzerin), die lüsternen Blicke der Nymphomanin (die Mutter), der neugierig-ängstliche Blick des kleinen Jungen. Dann die Blicke zwischen den Personen von Frau zu Frau, von Frau zu Mann, von Kind zu Frau, von Frau aus dem Fenster, von Kind in den Flur und auf den alten Etagenkellner. Der andere wird zum befragten und unverstandenen Spiegelbild, der Raum bleibt die schweigende Hülse, das Hotel die gemietete Gesamthülle, der Schutzraum, in dem man sich verkriecht. Die sexuellen Spannungen zwischen den Personen brechen immer wieder hervor wie aus einer anderen, unterschwelligen Welt. Sie sind archaische Kräfte, die unkontrolliert Körper und Geist befallen, giftig, voller perverser Abgründe. Triebe eben, sie bestimmen das Liegen, den Gang, das Stehen und die Blicke. Ohne diese Kräfte wäre das Leben vielleicht erträglich, wäre dieses Hotel vielleicht ein angenehmer Ort, so verwandelt er sich zunehmend zur Station einer Passion, kurz vor dem Ende, kurz vor der Kreuzigung. Es gibt keine Verständigung, die Worte reichen nicht – sie lügen – der Raum wird zur Falle, man kann sich in diesen Betten nur betrinken, noch tiefer in sich hineinfallenlassen oder den schnellen Sex suchen.

Space traps, eye traps, light traps. Space, bodies, light, shade, looks melt to form the film image. Atmosphere architecture. Mood built and turned into an image.
65. *The Last Laugh*, 1924; director: Friedrich Wilhelm Murnau, architecture: Robert Herlth and Walter Röhrig.
66. *The Maltese Falcon*, 1941, production and screenplay: John Huston, architecture: Robert Haas.
67. *Casablanca*, 1942; director: Michael Curtiz, architecture: Carl Jules Weyl (production design) and George James Hopkins (set decoration).
68. *The Big Sleep*, 1946; producer and director: Howard Hawks, architecture: Carl Jules Weyl (art director) and Fred M. MacLean (production design).

Raumfallen, Blickfallen, Lichtfallen. Raum, Körper, Licht, Schatten, Blicke verschmelzen zum Filmbild. Atmosphären-Architektur. Gebaute und zum Bild gewordene Stimmung.
65. *Der letzte Mann,* 1924; Regie: Friedrich Wilhelm Murnau, Architekur: Robert Herlth und Walter Röhrig.
66. *Die Spur des Falken,* 1941; Regie und Buch: John Huston, Architektur: Robert Haas.
67. *Casablanca,* 1942; Regie: Michael Curtiz, Architektur: Carl Jules Weyl (production design) und George James Hopkins (set decoration).
68. *Tote schlafen fest,* 1946; Produktion und Regie: Howard Hawks, Architektur: Carl Jules Weyl (art director) und Fred M. MacLean (production design).

Everyday rooms – kitchens, bedrooms, living-rooms, pool – refracted by film. The theatre-like stylization in early film architecture increasingly gives way to an approximation to everyday reality. Architectural fantasies remain the exception.
69. *Manpower*, 1941; director: Raoul Walsh, architecture: Max Parker.
70. *Glückskinder*, 1936; director: Paul Martin, architecture: Erich Kettelhut.
71. *Der Traum von Lieschen Müller* (or: *Happy-End im siebten Himmel*), 1961; director: Helmut Käutner, architecture: Otto Pischinger and Hertha Hareiter.
72. *Terms of Endearment*, 1983; screenplay, production and direction: James L. Brooks, architecture: Harold Michelson (art director), Polly Platt (production design) and Sandy Veneziano (set design).

Räume des Alltags – Küchen, Schlafzimmer, Wohnzimmer, Pool – in filmischer Brechung. Die theaterhafte Stilisierung der frühen Filmarchitekturen weicht zunehmend einer Angleichung an die Alltagsrealität. Architekturphantasien bleiben die Ausnahme.

69. *Herzen in Flammen,* 1941; Regie: Raoul Walsh, Architektur: Max Parker.

70. *Glückskinder,* 1936; Regie: Paul Martin; Architektur: Erich Kettelhut.

71. *Der Traum von Lieschen Müller* (oder: *Happy-End im siebten Himmel*), 1961; Regie: Helmut Käutner, Architektur: Otto Pischinger und Hertha Hareiter.

72. *Zeit der Zärtlichkeit*, 1983; Buch, Produktion und Regie: James L. Brooks, Architektur: Harold Michelson (art direktor), Polly Platt (production design) und Sandy Venziano (set design).

The great possibilities of film architecture lie in exaggeration, in unusual perspectives (from above, from below). The language extends from dull expression (prison-office-cell) via satirical emphasis to nightmarish spaces of delirium.
73. *Playtime*, 1967; screenplay and direction: Jacques Tati, architecture: Eugène Roman.
74. *M,* 1931, director: Fritz Lang, architecture: Emil Hasler and Karl Vollbrecht.
75. *The Trial*, 1962; director: Orson Welles, architecture: Jean Mandaroux (art director) and André Labussière (scenic artist).

In den Übertreibungen, den ungewöhnlichen Perspektiven, (von oben, von unten) liegen die großen Möglichkeiten der Filmarchitektur. Die Sprache reicht von dumpfer Expression (Gefängnis-Büro-Zelle), über satirische Zuspitzungen bis zu alptraumhaften Wahnräumen.
73. *Tatis herrliche Zeiten,* 1967; Buch und Regie: Jacques Tati, Architektur: Eugène Roman.
74. *M – Eine Stadt sucht einen Mörder,* 1931; Regie: Fritz Lang, Architektur: Emil Hasler und Karl Vollbrecht.
75. *Der Prozeß,* 1962; Buch und Regie: Orson Welles, Architektur: Jean Mandaroux (art director) und André Labussière (scenic artist).

76. *Shanghai-Express*, 1932; director: Josef von Sternberg, architecture: Hans Dreier. Marlene Dietrich in her compartment on the Shanghai-Express. Films set in trains seem to double the filmic idea: the train itself becomes a three-dimensional strip of film. Film in film in film.
77. *The Blue Angel*, 1930; director: Josef von Sternberg, architecture: Otto Hunte and Emil Hasler. Marlene Dietrich as naughty little Lola and Emil Jannings as Professor Unrat in Josef von Sternberg's *The Blue Angel*. Lola's dressing- room, cramped, and seeming to have been used for years, stuffed with things, furniture, props, glasses, little bottles, mirrors and curtains. A cramped little room that becomes an erotic trap.

76. *Shanghai–Express,* 1932; Regie: Josef von Sternberg, Architektur: Hans Dreier. Marlene Dietrich im Zugabteil des Shanghai-Expresses. Filme, die in den Zügen spielen, wirken wie eine Verdoppelung der filmischen Idee: Der Zug selbst wird zum dreidimensionalen Filmband. Film im Film im Film.
77. *Der blaue Engel,* 1930; Regie: Josef von Sternberg, Architektur: Otto Hunte und Emil Hasler. Marlene Dietrich als fesche Lola und Emil Jannings als Professor Unrat in *Der blaue Engel*. Lolas Garderobe, ein enger Raum, der wirkt als würde er seit Jahrzehnten benutzt, vollgestopft mit Dingen, Möbeln, Requisiten, Gläsern, Fläschchen, Spiegeln und Vorhängen. Eine enge Kammer, die zur erotischen Falle wird.

A room as a protective covering and vessel for fear. The architecture of the walls closes in, cuts things to pieces and determines people's relationships with each other.
78. *Key Largo*, 1948; director: John Huston, architecture: Leo Kuter and Fred M. MacLean.
79. *The Silence* (*Tystnaden*), 1963; screenplay and direction: Ingmar Bergman, architecture: P. A. Lundgren.

Raum als Schutzhülle und Angstgefäß. Die Architektur der Wände faßt zusammen, zerschneidet und bestimmt das Verhältnis der Personen untereinander.
78. *Hafen des Lasters / Gangster vor Key Largo,* 1948; Regie: John Huston, Architektur: Leo Kuter und Fred M. MacLean.
79. *Das Schweigen* (*Tystnaden*), 1963; Buch und Regie: Ingmar Bergman, Architektur: P. A. Lundgren.

Homes

An empty dwelling is at the centre of Bertolucci's film *Last Tango in Paris* (1972): these empty rooms are (like Bergman's hotel in *The Silence*) no-man's-land once more, and they take away the protagonists' inhibitions. They collide with each other in a physical and sexual way here that would never happen in a furnished dwelling. Perhaps for this reason: an individually furnished home requires responsibility and actions that can be repeated with a good conscience, but an empty house or flat demands daring and adventure.

The homes of film history reflect the history of modern architecture, and the way in which it is liked and disliked. In Hollywood films of the twenties and thirties there were any number of elegantly furnished modern homes that could have been designed by Richard Neutra or Le Corbusier. In reality none of the great architects (with the exception of Poelzig and Mallet-Stevens) ever worked for the cinema. Shabby interiors predominated in the forties.

The poverty and ruin of the post-war period can be discerned in films, in Marlene Dietrich's Berlin home in Billy Wilder's *A Foreign Affair* (1948), for example. In the fifties large, cleanly furnished homes start to appear, in Billy Wilder's *The Seven Year Itch* (1955), for example, and the little houses surrounded by lawns, with rooms that are far too cramped.

Constriction and space in houses are crucial for the lives of the people who live in them. The more they live on top of each other the greater is the danger of friction and quarrels. The more space there is around characters, the greater the danger of loneliness.

In Nicholas Ray's *Rebel without a Cause* (1955), Jimmy (James Dean) lives with his parents in a somewhat too cramped middle-class house. Inside we again see the narrow hall with the steep staircase leading upstairs, as in *Shadow of a Doubt*, but somewhat more confined, in fact overconfined. This is where the clash between father and son occurs. It is staged in such a way as though it were just a question of restricted space and having to come to terms with it. James Dean of course wants more, freedom of movement, inside and out. The father – as a weak looser, who has already taken far more blows than his son – has long since come to terms with the confined space, indeed sees it as a relative victory within a hard society. A director's greatness shows in the fact that – as is the case here with Nicholas Ray – there are certain moments at which we can understand everyone, Jimmy just as much as his father (particularly in the final scene), his mother, his girlfriend, who already looks like an adult who has conformed early, dreaming of children and this cramped house, and also the house itself, which stands there quietly and patiently, lets everything happen to it, and perhaps has its own dreams (of peace, emptiness, harmony or of love and music), but it was born deaf and dumb, and can never express a wish.

Middle-class furnished homes can be seen in countless fifties German, European and American films. The rebellion against this at the time of Woodstock and 1968 is also reflected in cinema homes. There are no more beds now, the mattresses are on the floor as in Godard's *Breathless* (1959) or Jean Eustache's *The Mother and the Whore* (1973).

Pretty Woman (1989) is interesting in terms of the eighties and nineties: here two homes are used to show the contrast between upper and lower classes. A prostitute lives with her friend in a cramped room above a pub. The room is stuffed full of dolls, cushions, souvenirs, rubbish and knick-knacks. One day a wealthy businessman lets her into his car in the street and takes her to a worldly apartment high over the city in the Beverly-Wilshire Hotel. After a number of adversities the story finally has a happy ending that can be equated with the rise of its principal character: she will be moving into even larger rooms, will wear even more elegant clothes, drive large cars and never again have to move back into her cramped accommodation.

Wohnungen

Eine leere Wohnung steht im Mittelpunkt von Bertoluccis Film *Der letzte Tango in Paris* (1972): Die leeren Räume sind (wie in Bergmans Hotel aus *Das Schweigen*) wieder Niemandsländer, die auf die handelnden Personen eine enthemmende Wirkung haben. Sie prallen hier körperlich-sexuell aufeinander, wie es in einer eingerichteten Wohnung nie geschehen würde. Vielleicht ist es so: Die individuell eingerichtete Wohnung fördert das verantwortliche und mit gutem Gewissen wiederholbare Handeln, die leere Wohnung dagegen das Wagnis und das Abenteuer.

In den Wohnungen der Filmgeschichte spiegelt sich die moderne Architekturgeschichte, die Zuneigung zu ihr und die Abneigung gegen sie. Im Hollywood-Film der zwanziger und dreißiger Jahre gibt es jede Menge elegant modern eingerichtete Wohnungen, die von Richard Neutra oder Le Corbusier entworfen sein könnten. In Wirklichkeit hat keiner der großen Architekten (mit Ausnahme von Poelzig und Mallet-Stevens) für den Film gearbeitet. In den vierziger Jahren überwiegen die schäbigen Interieurs.

Auch das Ärmliche und Ruinöse der Nachkriegszeit ist in den Filmen abzulesen, die Berliner Wohnung von Marlene Dietrich in Billy Wilders *A Foreign Affair* (1948) zum Beispiel. Mit den fünfziger Jahren tauchen die größeren, sauber eingerichteten Wohnungen auf, *Das verflixte 7. Jahr* (1955) von Billy Wilder, und die kleinen Häuschen im Grünen mit ihren viel zu engen Räumen.

Enge und Weite der Räume in den Häusern sind entscheidend für das Leben der Bewohner. Je enger die Menschen beieinander wohnen, um so größer die Gefahr von Reibung und Streit. Je größer der Raum um die Personen, desto größer die Gefahr der Einsamkeit.

In *Denn sie wissen nicht, was sie tun* (1955) von Nicholas Ray wohnt Jimmy (James Dean) mit seinen Eltern in einem etwas zu engen, bürgerlichen Haus. Innen sieht man wieder den schmalen Flur mit der steilen Treppe nach oben wie in *Im Schatten des Zweifels*, nur eben enger, etwas zu eng. Der Zusammenprall zwischen Vater und Sohn findet hier statt. Er ist so inszeniert, als ginge es um die Frage der räumlichen Beschränkung und des Sich-Damit-Abfinden-Müssens. James Dean will natürlich mehr, will die freie Bewegung, innen und außen. Der Vater hat sich – als weichlicher Verlierer, der schon weit mehr Schläge erhalten hat als sein Sohn – längst mit der Enge arrangiert, betrachtet sie sogar als relativen Sieg innerhalb einer harten Gesellschaft. Die Größe des Regisseurs zeigt sich darin, daß man – wie hier bei Nicholas Ray – in bestimmten Momenten jeden versteht, Jimmy genauso wie seinen Vater (Schlußzene vor allem), seine Mutter, seine Freundin (die bereits aussieht wie eine frühangepaßte Erwachsene, die von Kindern und diesem engen Haus träumt) und auch das Haus selbst, das still und duldsam dasteht, alles mit sich geschehen läßt, vielleicht auch seine Träume hat (von Stille, Leere, Harmonie oder von Liebe und Musik), jedoch taubstumm geboren wurde, niemals einen Wunsch äußern kann.

Die bürgerlich eingerichtete Wohnung gibt es in unzähligen Filmen der fünfziger Jahre im deutschen, europäischen wie im amerikanischen Film. Auch die Rebellion dagegen zur Zeit von Woodstock und 1968 spiegelt sich in den Kinowohnungen. Jetzt stehen hier keine Betten mehr, die Matratzen liegen auf dem Boden wie in *Außer Atem* (1959) von Godard oder in *Die Mama und die Hure* (1973) von Jean Eustache.

Für die achtziger und neunziger Jahre ist *Pretty Woman* (1989) interessant: Hier wird mit zwei Wohnungen der gesellschaftliche Gegensatz zwischen unten und oben gezeigt. Eine Prostituierte wohnt mit ihrer Freundin in einem engen Zimmer über einer Kneipe. Der Raum ist vollgestopft mit Puppen, Kissen, Andenken, Müll und Nippes. Eines Tages läßt sie ein reicher Geschäftsmann auf der Straße in sein Auto einsteigen und nimmt sie in ein mondänes Appartement mit, das hoch über der Stadt im Beverly Wilshire Hotel liegt. Nach vielen Widrigkeiten endet die Geschichte schließlich mit einem Happy-End, das den sozialen Aufstieg der Hauptdarstellerin nach sich zieht: Sie wird in noch größere Räume ziehen, immer elegantere Kleider tragen, große Autos fahren und nie mehr in ihre winzige Wohnung zurückkehren müssen.

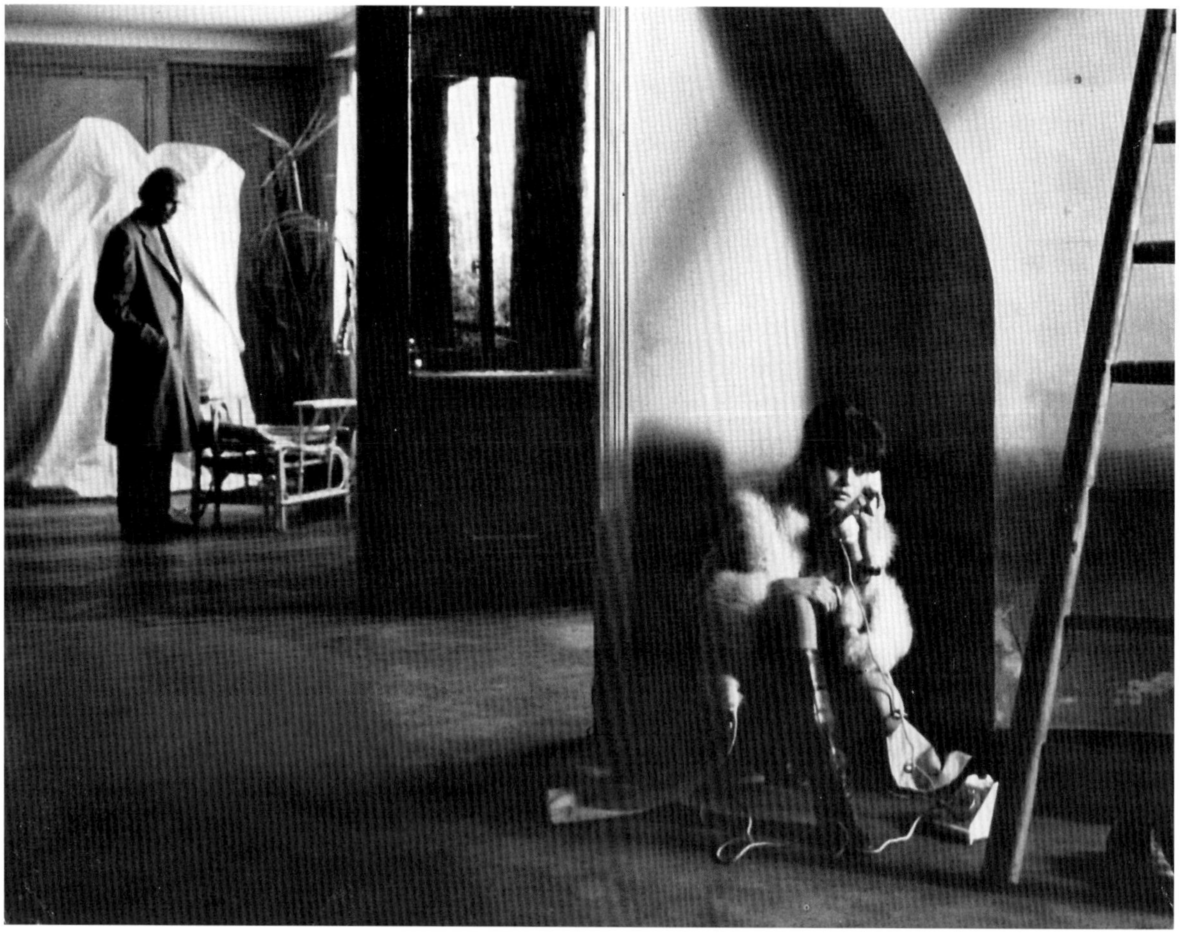

80. *Last Tango in Paris* (*L'Ultimo tango a Parigi / Le dernier tango à Paris*), 1972; director: Bernardo Bertolucci, architecture: Ferdinando Scarfiotti.
81. *The Mother and the Whore* (*La Maman et la putain*), 1973; director: Jean Eustache.
82. *Rebel without a Cause,* 1955; director: Nicholas Ray, architecture: William Wallace.

80. *Der letzte Tango in Paris* (*L'Ultimo tango a Parigi / Le dernier tango à Paris*), 1972; Regie: Bernardo Bertolucci, Architektur: Ferdinando Scarfiotti.
81. *Die Mama und die Hure* (*Le Mamam et la putain*), 1973; Regie: Jean Eustache.
82. *Denn sie wissen nicht, was sie tun,* 1955; Regie: Nicholas Ray, Architektur: William Wallace.

Darkening and lightening

Empty rooms are one thing, rooms used as accommodation another. There are countless stages and variations in between.

One route leads back to the caves and catacombs of *Metropolis* and *The Cabinet of Dr. Caligari*. Here we also find the laboratories of *Frankenstein* (1931) and the gloomy studio in Michael Curtiz's *Mystery of the Wax Museum* (1933). All horror films fit into this category. The rooms close down to become dangerous cave prisons from which it is possible to escape only at the last minute (if at all). This is where all threatened spaces in Hitchcock's films belong: the shower scene in *Psycho* and the Bodega Bay sittingroom with its doors and windows pecked to pieces in *The Birds*.

And then there are the prison cells, the passages and corridors in penitentiaries, the rooms and interrogations, the passages and sewers under the streets in Carol Reed's *The Third Man* (1949) and in Louis Malle's *Lift to the Scaffold* (1957).

The other route leads into the large, bright rooms of directors' suites, high over the city, as in *Wall Street* (1987). This film offers the possibility of penetrating all rooms in the city, observing people in their surroundings and thus understanding the possible ways in which society can be interwoven. The city, which normally shows itself as a closed system – almost all its rooms are taboo zones – drops its veils.

Verdüsterungen und Erhellungen

Die leeren Räume sind eine Sache. Die als Wohnungen benutzten Räume eine andere. Dazwischen gibt es unzählige Abstufungen und Variationen.

Der eine Weg führt in die Höhlen und Katakomben von *Metropolis* und das *Cabinet des Dr. Caligari* zurück. Hier liegen auch die Laborkammern in *Frankenstein* (1931) und das düstere Atelier in *Das Wachsfigurenkabinett* (1933) von Michael Curtiz. Alle Grusel- und Horrorfilme gehören hierher. Die Räume schließen sich zu gefährlichen Höhlengefängnissen, aus denen es nur im letzten Augenblick ein Entfliehen gibt (wenn überhaupt). Hierher gehören alle bedrohten Räume in den Filmen Hitchcocks: die Duschzelle in *Psycho* und das Bodega-Bay-Wohnzimmer mit den von Vögeln zerhackten Tür- und Fensterflügeln.

Dazu kommen die Gefängniszellen und die Gänge und Flure in den Strafanstalten, die Räume und Verhöre, die Gänge und Rohre unter der Stadt in *Der dritte Mann* (1949) von Carol Reed und in *Fahrstuhl zum Schafott* (1957) von Louis Malle.

Der andere Weg führt in die großen, hellen Räume der Führungsetagen, hoch über der Stadt, zum Beispiel in *Wallstreet* (1987). Der Film bietet die Möglichkeit, in alle Räume der Stadt einzudringen, die Personen in ihrer Umgebung zu beobachten und so das mögliche Geflecht der Gesellschaft zu durchschauen. Die Stadt, die sich normalerweise als geschlossenes System zeigt – fast alle Räume in ihr sind Tabuzonen –, läßt ihre Hüllen fallen.

83. *Frankenstein*, 1931; screenplay and direction: James Whale, architecture: Charles Hall.

83. *Frankenstein,* 1931; Buch und Regie: James Whale, Architektur: Charles Hall.

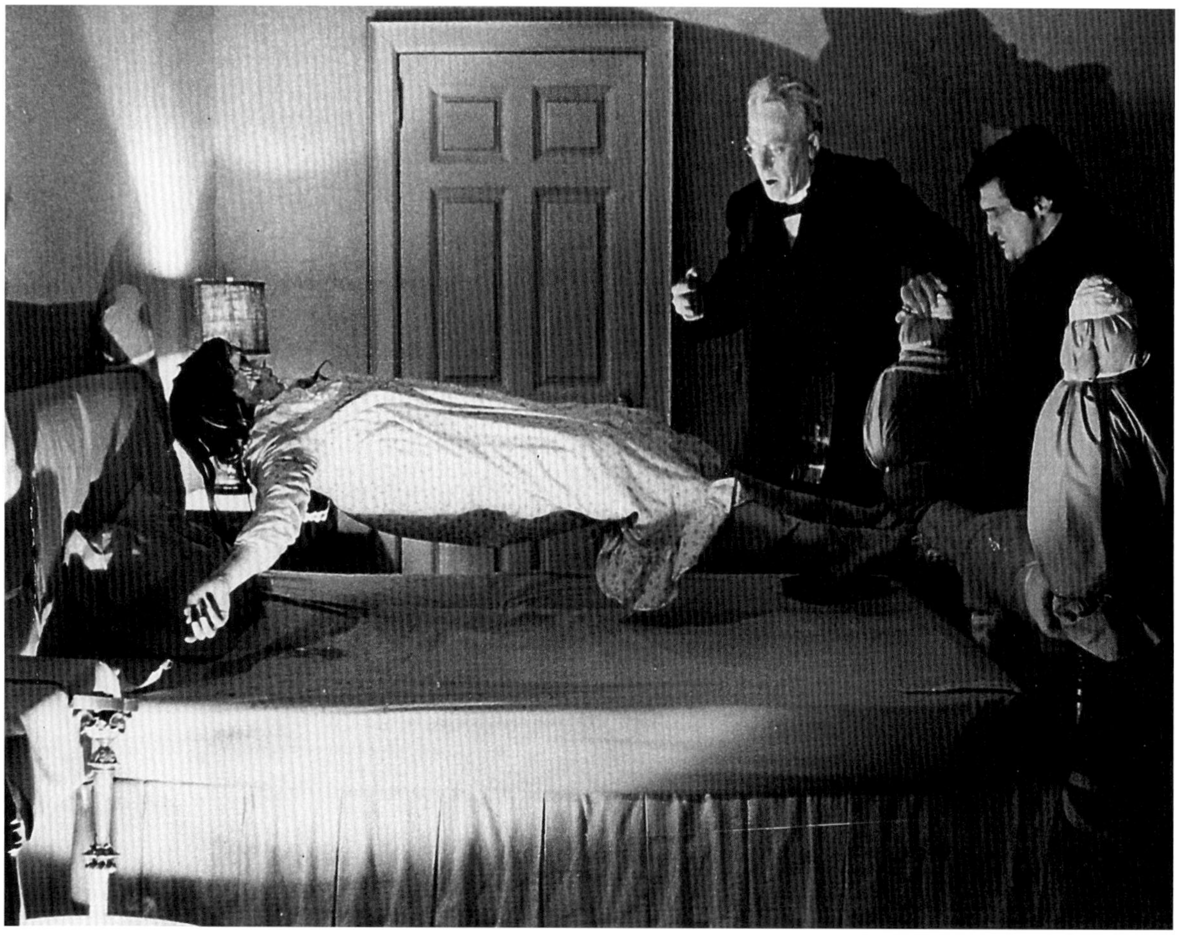

Horror rooms. Rooms of torture and cruel death. Nightmare rooms. In contrast, rooms of success and social betterment.
84. *No Answer from F. P. 1*, 1932; director: Karl Hartl, architecture: Erich Kettelhut.
85. *The Exorcist,* 1973; director: William Friedkin, architecture: Bill Malley.
86. *Wall Street,* 1987; director: Oliver Stone, architecture: Stephen Hendrickson, Leslie Bloom and Susan Bode (set decoration).

Horrorräume. Räume der Folter und des grausamen Sterbens. Alpträume. Dagegen die Räume des Erfolgs und des gesellschaftlichen Aufstiegs.
84. *F. P. 1 antwortet nicht,* 1932; Regie: Karl Hartl, Architektur: Erich Kettelhut.
85. *Der Exorzist,* 1973; Regie: William Friedkin, Architektur: Bill Malley.
86. *Wall Street,* 1987; Regie: Oliver Stone, Architektur: Stephen Hendrickson, Leslie Bloom und Susan Bode (set decoration).

Fittings and furnishings

Fittings and furnishings are to rooms as clothing is to actors. They reveal character. The furniture stands around, conspicuous or inconspicuous, old-fashioned or super-modern, and is used or gets in the way.

In comedy films, Laurel and Hardy, Charlie Chaplin, Buster Keaton or W.C. Fields it tends to be an obstacle, and distorts the handling of reality. It is often abused, stood on its head, sawn up, smashed, used as a boat or a car. The bed is the trickiest, of course.

Love does not have a large part to play in comedy films, it is more likely – as with Laurel and Hardy – that the bed will be used as a barbecue. Oliver Hardy pulls the mattress back, puts a fish on the metal grid and a lighted candle underneath. A little later the fish – admittedly somewhat shrunken – is ready to eat. The next problem is using the makeshift table that Stan Laurel has laid elegantly. As always, everything will end in disaster, with people, furnitures, tables, chairs and beds in a chaotic muddle.

The Marx Brothers use furniture as something alien as well. They lie under tables, stand on them, use tables and armchairs to build barricades, hang from lamps and swing around the room like Tarzan, slide down banisters and lie on cupboards.

We are often tempted to see buildings, towns, rooms and furniture as objects as such, detached from ownership and the people who use them, look after them, love them and hate them. In reality there is almost nothing that does not belong to someone or with which someone does not claim a relationship. To this extent the everyday view of these things is abbreviated and superficial. Painstakingly acquired information is needed to look beneath the surface. Film makes the tissue of relationships comprehensible.

People express themselves with their homes as they do with their clothing. This is an important aspect for some people, others merely glance at it contemptuously. In any case fittings and furnishings in films with their furniture and fabrics, knick-knacks and plants are ideal objects for studying the mood of the times.

Raumeinrichtungen und Möbel

Wohnungseinrichtungen und Möbel gehören zu den Häusern und Räumen wie Kleider zu den Schauspielern. Sie charakterisieren die Personen. Die Möbel stehen herum, unauffällig oder auffällig, altmodisch oder supermodern, sie werden benutzt oder versperren nur den Weg.

In den Filmen der Komiker, Stan und Ollie, Charlie Chaplin, Buster Keaton oder W.C. Fields bilden sie eher Hindernisse, verstellen den Umgang mit der Realität. Oft büßen sie ihren eigentlichen Zweck ein und werden auf den Kopf gestellt, zersägt, zertrümmert, als Schiff verwendet oder als Auto. Am heikelsten ist natürlich das Bett.

Die Liebe spielt bei den Komikern nicht die größte Rolle, schon eher verwandelt sich das Bett – wie bei Stan und Ollie – zum Grillplatz. Ollie schlägt die Matratze zurück, legt einen Fisch auf den Metallrost und stellt eine brennende Kerze unter das Gitter. Wenig später ist der Fisch – allerdings ziemlich geschrumpft – fertig zum Essen. Die nächsten Probleme ergeben sich bei der Benutzung des provisorischen Tisches, den Stan vornehm gedeckt hat. Alles wird – wie immer – in einer Katastrophe enden, bei der sich Menschen, Möbel, Tische, Stühle und Betten zu einem chaotischen Knäuel verschnüren.

Auch bei den Marx Brothers werden die Möbel oft befremdlich verwendet. Man versteckt sich unter Tischen, man stellt sich darauf, baut mit Tischen und Sesseln Barrikaden, hängt sich an Lampen und schwingt durch den Raum wie Tarzan, man rutscht Treppengeländer herunter und legt sich auf Schränke.

Bei Häusern, Städten, Räumen und Möbeln ist man oft verführt, sie als Objekte an sich zu betrachten, losgelöst von Besitz und Menschen, die sie benutzen, pflegen, lieben und hassen. In der Realität gibt es fast nichts, was nicht jemandem gehört oder von dem niemand behauptet, daß es Beziehungen zu ihm hätte. Insofern ist der alltägliche Blick auf diese Dinge verkürzt und oberflächlich. Hinter die Oberflächen zu schauen, ist nur nach mühsamer und langwieriger Information möglich. Durch den Film wird das Beziehungsgeflecht durchschaubar.

Die Bewohner drücken sich mit ihrer Wohnung aus wie mit ihrer Kleidung. Den einen ist dieser Aspekt wichtig, die anderen haben dafür nur verächtliche Blicke. In jedem Fall sind die Raumeinrichtungen der Filme, mit ihren Möbeln und Stoffen, ihren Nippes und ihren Pflanzen ideale Studienobjekte für eine Zeitstimmung.

87. *Mon Oncle,* 1958; screenplay and direction: Jacques Tati, architecture: Henri Schmitt.
88. *Playtime*, 1967; screenplay and direction: Jacques Tati, architecture: Eugène Roman.

87. *Mein Onkel* (*Mon Oncle*), 1958; Buch und Regie: Jacques Tati, Architektur: Henri Schmitt.
88. *Tatis herrliche Zeiten*, 1967; Buch und Regie: Jacques Tati, Architektur: Eugène Roman.

89. *Spies,* 1927/28; screenplay and direction: Fritz Lang, architecture: Otto Hunte and Karl Vollbrecht.
90. *Topper,* 1937; director: Norman Z. McLeod, architecture: W. L. Stevens, A. I. Royce and Alex de Sakhnoffsky.

89. *Spione*, 1927/28; Buch und Regie: Fritz Lang, Architektur: Otto Hunte und Karl Vollbrecht.
90. *Topper – Das blonde Gespenst*, 1937; Regie: Norman Z. McLeod, Architektur: W. L. Stevens, A. I. Royce und Alex de Sakhnoffsky.

Stairs

Stairs are popular places for encounters and clashes inside apartments and houses.

First come the back stairs. Gloomy, sinister areas of repressed emotion and social exclusion. Then they become larger and wider. They take us to Odessa and the great open steps of the *Battleship Potemkin* (1925) by Sergej Eisenstein, to revolution and to the famous pram rattling on its own down the countless steps. Sometimes they take us into fairy-tale and myth, as in the *Nibelungen* (1922–1924) by Fritz Lang), or into luxury hotels and possible social advancement, but often to erotic adventure as well. After an interlude with the show staircase lit from within, with the Radio City Music Hall dancers and the bathing beauties of the Hollywood revue films, we return to the psychological steps of the Black Series, private detectives and gangsters. Finally the broad staircase with the famous glass of milk in Hitchcock's *Notorious* (1946). Then there is the scene on the stairs described above in *Rebel without a Cause*. In Frank Capra's *Arsenic and Old Lace* (1941) the room in which almost the whole film is set is opened up by a staircase leading both up and down from it. The actual plot evolves on the ground floor: two old widows take in poor lodgers and later poison them with arsenic, on the assumption that they are doing them a good turn. Upstairs lives a madman, who keeps running upstairs for a military attack. His task is to take the corpses downstairs via the cellar steps at night and to bury them in »Panama«, as it is called in the film.

There are countless chases involving stairs, nowadays department store escalators and nondescript staircases in blocks of flats.

Treppen

Treppen sind innerhalb von Wohnungen und Häusern beliebte Orte der Begegnung und der Auseinandersetzung.

Erst sind es Hintertreppen. Dunkle, finstere Bereiche der verdrängten Gefühle und des gesellschaftlichen Abseits. Dann werden sie größer und breiter. Führen nach Odessa auf die große Freitreppe in *Panzerkreuzer Potemkin* (1925) von Sergej Eisenstein zur Revolution und zum berühmten Kinderwagen, der allein die zahllosen Stufen hinunterrappelt. Führen einerseits in märchenhaft-mythologische Bereiche wie in den *Nibelungen* (1922–1924) von Fritz Lang, andererseits ins Grandhotel zum möglichen gesellschaftlichen Aufstieg, aber auch zum erotischen Abenteuer. Nach dem Zwischenspiel der von innen beleuchteten Showtreppe, mit den Tänzerinnen der Radio City Music Hall und den hübschen Badenixen der Hollywood-Revuefilme, treten wieder die psychologischen Treppen der Schwarzen Serie, der Privatdetektive und der Gangster ins Bild. Schließlich die breite Treppe mit der berühmten Milchglas-Szene aus Hitchcocks *Weißes Gift / Berüchtigt* (1946). Dann die bereits beschriebene Treppenszene in *Denn sie wissen nicht, was sie tun*. In *Arsen und Spitzenhäubchen* (1941) von Frank Capra wird der Raum, in dem fast der ganze Film spielt, erweitert, indem aus dem Raum eine Treppe nach oben und eine nach unten führt. Im Erdgeschoß spielt sich die eigentliche Handlung ab: Zwei alte Witwen nehmen arme Untermieter auf und bringen sie später, in der Annahme, ihnen etwas Gutes getan zu haben, mit Arsen um. Oben wohnt ein Verrückter, der immer wieder zur militärischen Attacke die Treppe hochläuft. Seine Aufgabe ist es, die Leichen nachts über die Kellertreppe nach unten zu bringen und sie in »Panama«, wie es im Film heißt, zu vergraben.

Es gibt unzählige Verfolgungsszenen, die über Treppen führen, heute über die Rolltreppen der Kaufhäuser und die Allerweltstreppenhäuser der Wohnanlagen.

91. *The Battleship Potemkin* (*Bronenosez Potjemkin*), 1925; director: Sergej Eisenstein, architecture: Vasili Rakhals.

91. *Panzerkreuzer Potemkin* (*Bronenosez Potjemkin*), 1925; Regie: Sergej Eisenstein, Architektur: Wasili Rakhals.

92. *The Desperate Hours*, 1955; director: William Wyler, architecture: Hal Pereira and Joseph MacMillan Johnson, Sam Comer and Grace Gregory (set construction).
93. *Pretty Woman,* 1989; director: Garry Marshall, architecture: Albert Brenner.
94. *Sunset Boulevard,* 1950; director: Billy Wilder, architecture: Hans Dreier and John Meehan.

92. *An einem Tag wie jeder andere,* 1955; Regie: William Wyler, Architektur: Hal Pereira und Joseph Mac Millan Johnson, Sam Comer und Grace Gregory (set construction).
93. *Pretty Woman,* 1989; Regie: Garry Marshall, Architektur: Albert Brenner.
94. *Boulevard der Dämmerung,* 1950; Regie: Billy Wilder, Architektur: Hans Dreier und John Meehan.

Stairs up, stairs down. Stairs to heaven and stairs to hell. Stairs of happiness and stairs of misery. Walking up or down stairs make movement rhythmic. The body takes on a mechanical quality, like a machine. Fritz Lang took up this motif in *Spies*: »... the many little episodes in this film are the precisely meshing cogs of an excessively complicated plot mechanism. ... It is like being in an ultra-modern factory with the rapid belt of the plot running through it and with individual picture sections standing on the edge of the belt like mechanized workers, waiting to make a quick move with their hands.«[6]
95. *Star Wars,* 1977–; screenplay and direction: George Lucas, architecture: John Barry, Norman Reynolds and Leslie Dilley.
96. *Frankenstein,* 1931; screenplay and direction: James Whale, architecture: Charles Hall.
97. *Spies,* 1927/28; director: Fritz Lang, architecture: Otto Hunte and Karl Vollbrecht.

Treppen nach oben, Treppen nach unten. Himmelstreppen und Höllentreppen. Glückstreppen und Unglückstreppen. Das Gehen auf Treppen rhytmisiert die Bewegung. Der Körper erhält etwas Mechanisches wie eine Maschine. Fritz Lang hat dieses Motiv in *Spione* aufgegriffen: » ... die vielen kleinen Episoden dieses Films sind exakt ineinandergreifende Räder eines überkomplizierten Handlungswerkes. ... Es ist wie in einer ultramodernen Fabrik, durch die ein hastig laufendes Band der Handlung rollt und in der am Rande des Bandes einzelne Bildabschnitte wie mechanisierte Arbeiter stehen, um einen raschen Handgriff zu tun.«[6]
95. *Krieg der Sterne,* 1977–; Buch und Regie: George Lucas, Architektur: John Barry und Norman Reynolds und Leslie Dilley.
96. *Frankenstein,* 1931; Buch und Regie: James Whale, Architektur: Charles Hall.
97. *Spione,* 1927/28; Regie: Fritz Lang, Architektur: Otto Hunte und Karl Vollbrecht.

Film stairs between revolutionary mass movement and glamorous Broadway euphoria.
98: *Metropolis,* 1925/26; director: Fritz Lang, architecture: Otto Hunte, Erich Kettelhut and Karl Vollbrecht.
99. *Broadway Melody of 1938*, 1938; director: Roy del Ruth, architecture: Cedric Gibbons.

Die Film-Treppe zwischen revolutionärer Massenbewegung und glamouröser Broadway-Euphorie.
98. *Metropolis*, 1925/26; Regie: Fritz Lang, Architektur: Otto Hunte, Erich Kettelhut und Karl Vollbrecht.
99. *Broadway Melodie of 1938*, 1938; director: Roy del Ruth, Architektur: Cedric Gibbons.

Doors

Herman G. Weinberg reports: »Once Pickford stormed out the studio shouting: ›Doors! He's directing the doors! All he's interested in is the doors!‹«[7] Even if this seems somewhat exaggerated, it contains a great deal of truth: no film director made as much use of doors as Ernst Lubitsch. Every strand of plot comes to an end here. The door opens, the actor or actress steps into the room beyond it, the door closes again and the viewer remains outside. We are not told what happens inside the door, it is left to our imagination. The door becomes an architectural editor, but also a bearer of secrets and an erotically charged motif. The closing door gives the room and thus the plot a front and a back, and as viewers we feel that the room in the film is surrounded by other rooms, and that it shows only one aspect of the character and the architecture. The ambiguity and layered depth of a cabinet of mirrors.

In the dream symbolism the house stands for the body, the windows and doors represent its orifices, especially those of the sexual organs.

In Lubitsch's *Bluebeard's Eighth Wife* (1938) the curved passage between his door and her door is the neutral area within the crossing paths, chance encounters and exchange of matrimonial blows, but also the area of dynamic attacks ending at the other's door. If it remains closed, disaster threatens, if it opens, something is going to happen. Surprising opening of a door comes to mean rape.

At the end of Lubitsch's film *Angel* (1937) confused emotions are portrayed by a confusion of rooms and doors in the Grand Duchess's salon. Each of the three key figures, the husband, the lover and the wife (Angel) is in a room, then the doors open and there are encounters, intersections. The doors join in, they are like falling borders, constellations of possibilities. The door leading out of the salon conceals the still open conclusion. In a surprising twist, Angel joins up with her husband. We see the two of them from behind, approaching the opening door arm in arm. Beyond it lies a nostalgic journey to Vienna and then back to the everyday routine. Ernst Lubitsch's art as a director lies in breaking off at the right moment.

Türen

Herman G. Weinberg berichtet: »Einmal stürmte die Pickford aus dem Studio und schrie: ›Türen! Er ist der Regisseur der Türen! Ihn interessieren nur die Türen!‹«[7] Auch wenn diese Behauptung der Pickford übertrieben erscheint, enthält sie doch viel Wahrheit: Kein Filmregisseur hat die Türen als handelnde Objekte so intensiv eingesetzt wie Ernst Lubitsch. Jeder Handlungsstrang findet hier sein Ende. Die Tür öffnet sich, der Schauspieler oder die Schauspielerin tritt in das dahinterliegende Zimmer, die Tür schließt sich wieder, und der Zuschauer bleibt draußen. Was hinter der Tür geschieht, wird nicht erzählt, bleibt der Phantasie des Zuschauers überlassen. Die Tür wird zum architektonischen Filmschnitt, aber auch zum Geheimnisträger und zum erotisch aufgeladenen Motiv. Mit der sich schließenden Tür erhält der Raum und damit die Handlung eine Vorder- und eine Rückseite, und man fühlt als Zuschauer, daß der Filmraum umgeben ist von anderen Räumen, daß er nur einen Gesichtspunkt und einen Zustand der Person und der Architektur zeigt. Doppelbödigkeit, Tiefschichtigkeit eines Spiegelkabinetts.

In der Traumsymbolik bedeutet das Haus den Körper, die Fenster und Türen entsprechen den Körperöffnungen, insbesondere den Öffnungen der Geschlechtsorgane.

In *Blaubarts achte Frau* (1938) von Lubitsch ist der gebogene Flur zwischen seiner Tür und ihrer Tür der neutrale Bereich der sich kreuzenden Wege, der zufälligen Begegnungen und des ehelichen Schlagabtauschs, aber auch der Bereich dynamischer Attacken, die an der Tür des anderen ihr Ende finden. Bleibt diese länger verschlossen, droht Unheil, öffnet sie sich, wird etwas passieren. Das überraschende Türöffnen enthält die Bedeutung einer Vergewaltigung.

Am Schluß des Films *Engel* (1937), ebenfalls von Lubitsch, wird die Verwirrung der Gefühle verdeutlicht durch einen Raum- und Türenwirrwarr im Salon der Großfürstin. Jede der drei entscheidenden Figuren, der Ehemann, der Liebhaber und die Ehefrau (Angel), befindet sich in einem Zimmer, dann öffnen sich die Türen, es kommt zu Begegnungen, Überkreuzungen. Die Türen sprechen mit, sie sind wie fallende Grenzen, Möglichkeitskonstellationen. Die Ausgangstür des Salons birgt den noch offenen Schluß. In einer überraschenden Wendung schließt sich Angel ihrem Ehemann an. Man sieht die beiden von hinten Arm in Arm auf die sich öffnende Tür zugehen. Dahinter liegt eine nostalgische Reise nach Wien und dann wieder der normale Alltagstrott. Die Kunst Lubitschs besteht darin, im richtigen Moment abzubrechen.

100. *Bluebeard's Eighth Wife*, 1938; director: Ernst Lubitsch, architecture: Hans Dreier and Robert Usher.

100. *Blaubarts achte Frau*, 1938; Regie: Ernst Lubitsch, Architektur: Hans Dreier und Robert Usher.

Windows

Windows are places of communication between private and public, between what is hidden and what is shown. A look through them can be innocent (information about the weather) or full of longing, can be about waiting, or full of hope or despair, or exclusion. Someone who is hiding observes through the window the strange events in the street (at the beginning of Hitchcock's *Shadow of a Doubt*, for example). Someone wanting to make contact with the street, the window or the house opposite will show himself, draw attention to himself by actions or gestures. Open windows indicate that the people who live there are in, closed windows – perhaps with the blinds down – suggest that there is no-one there, or that the residents are asleep. Open houses, closed houses. Windows are the house's eyes, behind them lurk the eyes of the people who live there.

In Alfred Hitchcock's *Rear Window* (1954) the filmgoer sees James Stewart with a broken leg, sitting in a wheelchair by the window overlooking the yard, and looking at the yard itself and the windows in the surrounding façades. As he can hardly move he looks out of the window almost all the time. Slowly individual fates start to emerge from the lives he observes, until finally the man opposite murders and dismembers his wife. The culprit has a sense of being watched and caught and gets into the voyeur's room. It is the archetypal fear of the voyeur: that suddenly distant, outside reality will become real, strike threateningly and come so close as to endanger life.

Fenster

Fenster sind Orte der Kommunikation zwischen dem Privaten und dem Öffentlichen, zwischen dem Verborgenen und dem Gezeigten. Von hier aus werden harmlose Blicke geworfen (Information über das Wetter) oder sehnsuchtsvolle Blicke, Blicke des Wartens, des Hoffens, aber auch Blicke der Verzweiflung und des Ausgeschlossenseins. Derjenige, der sich versteckt, beobachtet durch das Fenster die merkwürdigen Vorgänge auf der Straße, zum Beispiel am Anfang von Hitchcocks *Im Schatten des Zweifels*. Derjenige, der mit der Straße, dem Fenster und dem Haus gegenüber Kontakt aufnehmen will, zeigt sich, macht durch auffällige Aktionen auf sich aufmerksam. Offene Fenster weisen darauf hin, daß die Bewohner anwesend sind, geschlossene – vielleicht mit heruntergelassenen Rolläden – darauf, daß niemand da ist oder daß die Bewohner schlafen. Offene Häuser, geschlossene Häuser. Fenster sind die Augen des Hauses, hinter ihnen lauern die Augen der Bewohner.

In dem Film *Das Fenster zum Hof* (1954) von Alfred Hitchcock beobachtet der Kinobesucher James Stewart, der mit einem gebrochenen Bein im Rollstuhl am Fenster zum Hof sitzt und diesen Hof, die umgebenden Fassaden mit ihren Fenstern beobachtet. Da er sich kaum bewegen kann, schaut er fast ständig aus dem Fenster. Langsam entstehen aus Bruchstücken von beobachtetem Leben Einzelschicksale, bis schließlich der Mann von gegenüber seine Frau umbringt und zerstückelt. Der Täter fühlt sich ertappt und dringt in das Zimmer des Voyeurs ein. Es ist die archetypische Angst des Voyeurs, daß plötzlich die ferne, außerhalb liegende Realität tatsächlich real wird, bedrohlich zuschlägt und lebensgefährlich nahe rückt.

101, 102. *Rear Window,* 1954; screenplay, production and direction: Alfred Hitchcock, architecture: Hal Pereira and Joseph MacMillan Johnson.

101, 102. *Das Fenster zum Hof,* 1954; Buch, Produktion und Regie: Alfred Hitchcock, Architektur: Hal Pereira und Joseph MacMillan Johnson.

Visions

Film is also the image and space medium in which world situations, human history and urban history can be thought through to a conclusion. How will we be living in 50, in 100, in 500, in 1,000 years? Will there still be villages, cities, countryside? What about the animals? Science Fiction's particular field is life in space, in space stations, on the moon and other planets. *2001*: *A Space Odyssey, Star Wars* and *Alien* have already been mentioned. Urban Utopias have also been mentioned before (*Blade Runner*). Two interesting films of this kind were staged and produced in Hollywood in the last years: Steven Spielberg's *Jurassic Parc* (1993) and *Waterworld* (1995) by Kevin Reynolds and Kevin Costner.

Jurassic Parc tells a story in which it is reported that long-extinct creatures have survived or been reawakened on a lonely South Sea Island: dinosaurs. A Utopia of paradise, perhaps, of the primeval condition recreated. But this confrontation of man and animal is not without its dangers, and leads to threatening incidents. The film is intellectually refracted and enhanced by the fact that the reawakened dinosaurs were generated by complicated computer programs, and have thus returned to earth only virtually.

The story told in *Waterworld* is similarly simple, but – like all great Hollywood films – it is based on archetypal, mythical and universally valid fears and hopes: we are in the year 2500, and the world's ice-caps have melted completely. Sea level has risen so high that there is no land above it. There is only the sea left. All cities have been eradicated and are at the bottom of the sea: Manhattan, Hong Kong, Hamburg and Sidney, Los Angeles, Tokyo and Rio de Janeiro. The sea becomes a gigantic, slightly vaulted grey-green canvas that is completely empty. Art and civilization have collapsed. The few people who have survived live on lonely ships as pirates or have formed themselves into groups and built little floating cities. The film deals with a lonely pirate played by Kevin Costner, and a city-atoll that protects itself from the outside world with violence. This atoll is interesting architecturally. It does not represent a perfect technical world, but seems to have been flung together like a monstrous slum: »We wanted to use all the things that were floating in the water, like plastic products from old garbage dumps. We knew that that would be essential for the city itself. The range of colours was derived from the knowledge that everything that is in water for a long time changes from its original shape and qualities. Algae, salt and other organic things would influence its appearance – that meant that the colours we used had to be in shades of green and brown.«[8]

The atoll spells out everything in a new way: Stonehenge, Forum Romanum, Palais Royal, bodged together from shabby sheets of metal and cheap plastic sheeting. »The whole film revolves around a world made up of remains from many different but familiar cultures, all mixed in a cosmic mixer.«[9]

From this point there will be only floating cities, floating detached houses and trams. It will no longer be possible to set foot on dry land, unless a small paradise island is discovered somewhere, like by Kevin Costner at the end of the film, which, after a search for locations all over the world was shot on the island of Hawaii. The atoll, which was finally floated in Kawaihae harbour, was 110 metres in diameter and had a circumference of 400 metres. It could be rotated, and could be towed out to the open sea. The architecture was so expensive that it made *Waterworld* the costliest film ever produced.

Visionen

Film ist auch das Bild- und Raum-Medium, in welchem Weltzustände, menschliche Geschichte und Stadtgeschichte zu Ende gedacht werden kann. Wie leben wir in 50, wie in 100, wie in 500, wie in 1000 Jahren? Wird es dann noch Dörfer, Städte und Landschaften geben? Was ist mit den Tieren? Der Science-Fiction-Film befaßt sich vor allem mit dem Leben im Weltall, in Raumstationen, auf dem Mond und anderen Planeten. *2001: Odyssee im Weltall*, *Krieg der Sterne* und *Alien – Das unheimliche Wesen aus einer fremden Welt* ist bereits erwähnt worden. Auch von den Stadtutopien wurde bereits gesprochen (*Blade Runner*). In den letzten Jahren wurden in Hollywood zwei interessante Filme zu diesem Thema inszeniert und produziert: Steven Spielbergs *Jurassic Parc* (1993) und *Waterworld* (1995) von Kevin Reynolds und Kevin Costner.

In *Jurassic Parc* wird eine Geschichte erzählt, die davon berichtet, daß auf einer einsamen Südseeinsel längst ausgestorbene Tiere überlebt haben oder wieder zum Leben erweckt worden sind: die Dinosaurier. Eine Utopie des Paradieses vielleicht, des wiedererstandenen Urzustandes. Die Begegnung von Mensch und Tier ist jedoch nicht ungefährlich und führt zu bedrohlichen Konfrontationen. Da die wiederbelebten Dinosaurier komplizierten Computerprogrammen entstammen, also nur virtuell auf die Erde zurückgekehrt sind, erhält der Film eine intellektuelle Brechung und Überhöhung.

Die Geschichte, die in *Waterworld* erzählt wird, ist ähnlich einfach, berührt jedoch – wie alle großen Hollywoodfilme – archetypische, mythische und allgemeingültige Ängste und Hoffnungen: Wir befinden uns im Jahr 2500, alle Eiskappen der Welt sind geschmolzen. Der Meeresspiegel ist so hoch angestiegen, daß ihn kein Land der Erde mehr überragt. Es gibt nur noch das Meer. Alle Städte sind ausgelöscht und liegen am Meeresgrund: Manhattan, Hongkong, Hamburg und Sidney, Los Angeles, Tokio und Rio de Janeiro. Das Meer wird zu einer riesigen, leicht gewölbten grau-grünen Leinwand, die vollkommen leer ist. Kunst und Zivilisation sind untergegangen. Die wenigen Menschen, die überlebt haben, hausen als Piraten auf einsamen Schiffen oder haben sich in Gruppen zusammengeschlossen und kleine schwimmende Städte gebaut. Der Film handelt von einem einsamen Piraten, der von Kevin Costner verkörpert wird, und einem Stadtatoll, das sich gewalttätig gegen alle anderen abschirmt. Dieses Atoll ist architektonisch interessant. Es stellt keine perfekte Technikwelt dar, sondern erscheint als ein slumartig zusammen gewürfeltes Ungetüm: »Wir wollten all die Dinge nutzen, die im Wasser schwammen, zum Beispiel die Plastikprodukte von alten Müllkippen. Wir wußten, daß das unerläßlich für die Stadt selbst sein würde. Die Farbpalette wurde aus dem Wissen abgeleitet, daß alles, was lange Zeit im Wasser ist, sich in der ursprünglichen Form und Beschaffenheit ändert. Algen, Salz und andere organische Dinge würden das Aussehen beeinflussen – das bedeutete, daß die Farben, die wir benutzten, einen grünen und braunen Farbton haben mußten.«[8]

Das Atoll buchstabiert alles neu: Stonehenge, Forum romanum, Palais Royal, aus schäbigen Blechbahnen und billigen Kunststoffplatten zusammengezimmert. »Der ganze Film dreht sich um eine Welt, die aus den Überresten vieler verschiedener, jedoch vertrauter Kulturen besteht, die alle mit einem kosmischen Mixer vermischt sind.«[9]

Ab jetzt wird es nur noch schwimmende Städte geben, schwimmende Einfamilienhäuser und Straßenbahnen. Man wird keinen Fuß mehr auf trockenes Land setzen können, es sei denn, man entdeckt noch irgendwo eine kleine paradiesische Insel, wie Kevin Costner am Ende des Films, der, nachdem die ganze Welt nach Drehorten abgesucht worden war, auf der Insel Hawaii gedreht wurde. Das Atoll, das schließlich im Hafen von Kawaihae schwamm, hatte einen Durchmesser von 110 und einen Umfang von 400 Metern. Es war drehbar und konnte auf das offene Meer hinausgezogen werden. Die Architektur war so aufwendig, daß *Waterworld* als der teuerste Film gilt, der je produziert wurde.

103. *Waterworld,* 1995; director: Kevin Reynolds, architecture: Dennis Gassner.

103. *Waterworld,* 1995; Regie: Kevin Reynolds, Architektur: Dennis Gassner.

pp. 100, 101
104–109. *Star Wars*, 1977–; director: George Lucas, architecture: John Barry, Norman Reynolds and Leslie Dilley.

S. 100, 101
104–109. *Krieg der Sterne*, 1977–; Regie: George Lucas, Architektur: John Barry, Norman Reynolds und Leslie Dilley.

Interplay

We can only speculate about whether there has really been interplay between film architecture and real, used architecture in the hundred years since the medium of film has existed.

Expressionist film architecture was strongly influenced by painting and sculpture. Rooms painted in an Expressionist manner were in existence ten years before the films. Some Expressionist architects' attempts to film their own visions all failed.

This is particularly true of Bruno Taut's attempt to stage his *Weltbaumeister*. The urban Utopias of the *Metropolis* film are more difficult. On the one hand they make the exisiting American skyscraper city part of the vision – Fritz Lang had seen the Manhattan skyline on his 1924 trip to America –, on the other hand these skyscraper cities were raised by exaggeration to a monumental and gigantic scale that took them on to the frightening plane of Science Fiction. Besides it is later possible to see that Fascist order structures are being anticipated here.

In America twenties and thirties film architecture followed the developments of the International Style very closely. Whether it invented its own images in doing this is a matter of dispute. The similarity of many of Richard Neutra's interiors and some film interiors has already been pointed out. Some of Modern architecture's favourite devices – streamlining, ship's decks, machines, elegant disguise, whiteness and a metallic quality – crop up in countless films of the period.

Certainly in America there was an interplay between the magnificent thirties musicals and the emergence of marble Art déco lobbies. Whether Hollywood's Black Series also influenced American interior décor is rather more doubtful. But these films certainly had a great influence on clothes and hairstyles, to say nothing of ways of smoking or sitting down in armchairs.

The majority of films produced today largely follow built and lived reality in their architecture and décor. Many film architects photograph certain yards and parts of streets so that they can be copied as realistically as possible in the studio. Of course this applies to films set in the present day. Films set in the fifties or earlier are given a suitable period backdrop.

Seen in this way the visionary power of film architecture is limited to a very few productions, which have made this vision their subject, e. g. *Brazil* (1984), *Batman* (1989) or *Blade Runner* (1982).

Despite this, film architecture and film rooms have instilled a new awareness of buildings and homes into people's heads. The powerful influence of the world-wide effect of Hollywood films in particular can never be fully assessed. Since audience figures for individual films have approached the billion mark (Spielberg's *Jurassic Parc* even went past it), this medium (together with television) has provided the possibility of a world architecture – even if it is imaginary. Every filmgoer who has seen *Pretty Woman*, for example, now thinks he knows what a suite in Hollywood's Beverly-Wilshire Hotel looks like. But we can only speculate about how many actual dreams about home life it stimulated.

Wechselwirkungen

Ob es in den hundert Jahren, seitdem es das Medium Film gibt, zu wirklichen Wechselwirkungen zwischen Filmarchitektur und realer, benutzter Architektur gekommen ist, darüber läßt sich spekulieren.

Die expressionistische Filmarchitektur wurde stark von der Malerei und der Bildhauerei beeinflußt. Expressionistisch gemalte Räume gab es schon zehn Jahre vor den Filmen. Versuche einiger expressionistischer Architekten, eigene Visionen zu verfilmen, schlugen alle fehl.

Das gilt vor allem für das Projekt von Bruno Taut, seinen *Weltbaumeister* in Szene zu setzen. Schwieriger verhält es sich mit den Stadtutopien des *Metropolis*-Films. Einerseits setzte man die bereits existierende amerikanische Wolkenkratzerstadt in die Vision ein – Fritz Lang hatte die Kulisse Manhattans bereits 1924 auf einer Amerikareise gesehen –, andererseits wurden diese Wolkenkratzerstädte durch die Übertreibung ins Monumental-Gigantische auf eine beängstigende Science-fiction-Ebene gehoben. Außerdem konnte man später sehen, daß hier faschistische Ordnungsstrukturen vorweggenommen worden sind.

In Amerika hat sich die Film-Architektur der zwanziger und dreißiger Jahre stark an den Entwicklungen des Internationalen Stils orientiert. Ob sie dabei eigene Bilder erfunden hat, darüber gehen die Meinungen auseinander. Die Ähnlichkeit zwischen manchen Innenräumen Richard Neutras und manchen Film-Interieurs wurde bereits hervorgehoben. Einige Vorlieben der modernen Architektur – die Stromlinie, das Schiffsdeck, die Maschine, das elegant Verkleidete, das Weiße und das Metallische – tauchen in zahlreichen Filmen dieser Zeit auf.

Sicher gab es in Amerika eine Wechselwirkung zwischen den prunkvollen Musical-Filmen der dreißiger Jahre und der Entstehung marmorner Art-Déco-Lobbies. Ob die Schwarze Serie Hollywoods auch auf die Wohnungseinrichtung der Amerikaner Einluß hatte, ist eher zu bezweifeln. Was die Kleidung und die Frisuren betraf, so war der Vorbildcharakter dieser Filme bestimmt stark, ganz zu schweigen von der Art zu rauchen oder sich in den Sessel zu setzen.

Die Mehrzahl der heute produzierten Filme orientiert sich in Architektur und Ausstattung weitgehend an der gebauten und gelebten Realität. Viele Filmarchitekten photographieren bestimmte Hinterhöfe und Straßenteile, um sie dann im Atelier möglichst realistisch nachbauen zu lassen. Das gilt natürlich nur für Filme, die die heutige Zeit zum Thema haben. Filme, die in den fünfziger Jahren oder gar noch früher spielen, erhalten ihr zeitlich passendes Outfit.

So gesehen ist die visionäre Kraft der Filmarchitekturen auf wenige Produktionen beschränkt, die sich diese Vision zum Thema gemacht haben, zum Beispiel *Brazil* (1984), *Batman* (1989) oder *Blade Runner* (1982).

Dennoch hat sich mit den Film-Architekturen und Film-Räumen ein neues Bewußtsein von Gebautem und Bewohntem in die Köpfe der Menschen eingeschlichen. Die weltweite Wirkung vor allem der Hollywoodfilme läßt sich in ihrem machtvollen Einfluß nur erahnen. Seitdem sich die Besucherzahlen der einzelnen Filme der Milliardengrenze angenähert, bei Spielbergs *Jurassic Parc* sogar bereits überschritten haben, hat man mit diesem Medium (in Zusammenhang mit dem Fernsehen) zum ersten Mal in der Menschheitsgeschichte die Möglichkeit zu einer – wenn auch imaginären – Weltarchitektur. Jeder Filmbesucher, der zum Beispiel *Pretty Woman* gesehen hat, glaubt jetzt zu wissen, wie eine Hotelsuite im Beverly-Wilshire-Hotel in Hollywood aussieht. Wieviel tatsächliche Wohnungsträume davon angeregt wurden, darüber kann man nur spekulieren.

110. *Across the Pacific*, 1942; director: John Huston, architecture: Robert Haas and Hugh Reticker.

110. *Abenteuer in Panama,* 1942; Regie: John Huston, Architektur: Robert Haas und Hugh Reticker.

111, 112. *Blade Runner*, 1982; director: Ridley Scott, architecture: David Snyder (art director), Lawrence G. Pauli (production designer) and Syd Mead (visual futurist).
113. *Dick Tracy,* 1990; producer and director: Warren Beatty, architecture: Harold Michelson (art director) and Richard Sylbert (production designer).

111, 112. *Blade Runner,* 1982; Regie: Ridley Scott, Architektur: David Snyder (art director), Lawrence G. Pauli (production designer) und Syd Mead (visual futurist).
113. *Dick Tracy,* 1990; Produktion und Regie: Warren Beatty, Architektur: Harold Michelson (art director) und Richard Sylbert (production designer).

Film reality and studio fiction

No scene of *Casablanca* was actually filmed in Africa. The whole film was shot from early May to late July 1942 in the Warner Studios at 4000 Warner Boulevard in Burbank, North Hollywood, on Stage 9 and Stage 21.

Any interested filmgoer today knows that the fictional world of film is created in the studio using architectural fragments, models, back projections, mirror tricks, painted backdrops, large-format photographs and virtually generated settings.

There are numerous films that concern themselves with this fringe area of reality, with this world of studio fiction. Here people talk of a glimpse behind the scenes, but this too can only be faked, as there is a second crew behind the one being filmed that ultimately remains invisible. Despite all this it always seems like a moment of truth when Fellini or Hitchcock puts in a personal appearance. In Truffaut's *Night for Day* (1972/73) the rear of the architectural setting is expressly shown. The filmgoer is intended to see how difficult it is to produce apparent reality and what a schizophrenic life an actor leads: life does not equal life. Genuine life and acted life run separately from each other and often complement each other. The director takes on god-like qualities: he has all the threads in his hand and knows what will happen in these rooms and outside these buildings in the next few hours, what will be said, what emotions will emerge and which facial expressions will be seen. Reality – even though fictitious – as a time-space that can be planned.

In Fellini's *Eight and a Half* it is not just the fiction of the film setting that is broken open here, but also the fiction of imagination and thinking. All realities and fictions swirl around together in the film-director's head. He wants to capture them and fix them in a screenplay and a film. The process by which a film emerges is shown as an autobiographical crisis. Every observation and every idea brings a chain of images from associations and memories.

Hotel, spa, drinking-hall, spa concert, fragments of city and landscape. The common link is the film set. In *Eight and a Half* Fellini stages a ballet of bodies, faces, sentences, thoughts and scraps of conversation to music by Wagner and Rossini. Stories are dabbed on. Surfaces. Every face and every object becomes part of the new fiction that is emerging. Every strand of spaghetti becomes a thread in Ariadne's web. But the path-system that is opening up remains puzzling, staggers from image to image. Association waltz and memory tango. Does the past explain now or now the past? There are no answers, the questions wobble out of the picture, possible answers are spoken beyond the film. Memories surge up in sensuous images and become entangled in the architecture of the rooms. Reality is not reality. There are other surfaces under the surface. Things are smashed up and put together again. Skins are shed. Images. Fellini shows the process of film creation as a crazy blend of autobiography, memory, observation, description and fantastic exaggeration. Architecture remains a possible link, a possible vessel without which the splinters of plot would fly apart once and for all.

This slipping from one world into another has become a subject in its own right. More and more people want to see the transition and take guided tours of studios in Hollywood, Berlin and Geiselgasteig in their thousands. It is a remarkable experience for everyone not to see the city itself any more but nothing but hollow façades. The seriousness with which reality is copied here, but as an empty shell, without function, produces an uneasy feeling. In these film streets the visitor feels afraid at how easily the city can be sucked dry, degenerating into a rigid mask, a mummy, a stuffed creature. We recognize with dismay that these outer skins are enough, and that perhaps the real city is a lie, a fiction. What should we hold on to?

Today film fiction has been joined by television fiction. All the films ever made are shown there, again and again. It was not until this is possible that filmed images secured the kind of dominant place in viewers' heads that they did not have previously.

More television films are shot than cinema films in the world's great studios today. But the problems have remained essentially the same.

Perhaps soap operas are as important for current everyday reality as visits to the market or bridge club used to be. They extend our everyday space and our circle of friends and acquaintances. Everyone involved also has a window opening on to Coronation Street or Dallas.

Perhaps detective films are German television's most important contribution in the past twenty years. In a hundred years these films will reflect our age in just the same way as the Hollywood Black Series reflected the forties. Black-and-white stylization is no longer a feature, but sophisticated lighting techniques make up for this by creating a strange artificiality in the rooms.

The murder they portray and its painstaking solution always takes place in another town. Usually the incident takes place in the upper echelons of society, an opportunity to show fashionably cool interiors: intrigues are spun in these overlighted and uncomfortable houses with view of a pool or an extensive garden that are intended to checkmate the competitors. But – as always – the intriguers are entangled in their own net. Often they are in fact not the murderer – that needs a culprit who is more wicked and unscrupulous – but all of them would have been in a position to commit a murder.

It is not enough to portray a society by filming it from the outside, its murky depths and perversions have to be part of the picture as well. A criminal case is best suited to this. It is like throwing a stone into the water and then carefully following the waves and the way in which it sinks. Tension as a whirlpool and funnel into which the characters are drawn is important for dramatic structure. The ancient Greeks knew that, and so did Hollywood directors at a later stage.

The structure is always similar: you take a plot that runs in a straight line, cut it into fifty individual pieces and put it together like a jigsaw puzzle, so that the complete, comprehensible picture is not revealed until the last moment (enlightenment).

This fragmentation also corresponds roughly to the Black Series: it is always a question of controlled doses of knowledge and information. For as long as I know people I get to know what they are doing, and then a tissue of suppositions and suspicions, everyone against everyone else, emerges. All the pent-up hatred comes to the surface, the rage, and also suppressed love. Recognition of the truth, the true state of affairs, is the object. Seen in this way detective films and scenes of crime are enlightenment films. The detective inspector as an undercover Faust?

The fact that death is central – unnatural death, murder – gives these films an extreme quality. They go to the ultimate limit.

Alongside the enlightenment rituals the viewer also learns a great deal about rooms in this society: what a police station looks like, a prison cell, an interrogation room, a court, the detective's home, a model's home, a successful businessman's home etc. As all this is provided together with clothing, speech, opinions and faces it produces an image of society, today, now. We can compare these images with reality and draw our conclusions.

There are similar series and phenomena all over the world.

Film-Realität und Studio-Fiktion

Für den Film *Casablanca* wurde nicht eine einzige Szene in Afrika gedreht. Der gesamte Film entstand in den Warner Studios am Warner Boulevard Nr. 4000 in Burbank, North Hollywood, auf der Bühne 9 und der Bühne 21 zwischen Anfang Mai und Ende Juli 1942.

Jeder interessierte Filmbesucher weiß heute darüber Bescheid, daß in den Studios der Welt die Fiktion der Filme über Architekturfragmente, über Modell, Rückprojektionen, Spiegeltricks, gemalte Kulissen, Großphotos und virtuell produzierte Kulissen hergestellt wird.

Es gibt zahlreiche Filme, die sich mit dieser Grenzzone der Wirklichkeit, mit dieser Studio-Fiktionswelt beschäftigen. Vom berühmten Blick hinter die Kulissen ist die Rede, der allerdings auch nur vorgetäuscht sein kann, weil hinter der gefilmten Crew eine zweite, unsichtbare steht, die letztlich unsichtbar bleibt. Trotz allem erscheint es immer wieder wie ein Moment der Wahrheit, wenn Fellini oder Hitchcock persönlich ins Bild treten. In Truffauts *Amerikanischer Nacht* (1972/73) werden die Rückseiten der Architekturkulissen ausführlich gezeigt. Der Zuschauer soll sehen, wie schwierig die Produktion scheinbarer Wirklichkeit ist und wie schizophren das Leben eines Schauspielers abläuft: Leben ist nicht gleich Leben. Echtes Leben und gespieltes Leben laufen nebeneinander her und widersprechen sich oft. Der Regisseur gerät in die Nähe des lieben Gottes, der die Fäden in der Hand hat und der weiß, was in diesen Räumen, vor diesen Hausfassaden in den nächsten Stunden ablaufen wird, welche Sätze fallen, welche Emotionen auftauchen und welche Gesichtsausdrücke sich zeigen werden. Realität – wenn auch fiktiv – als planbarer Zeitraum.

In Fellinis *Achteinhalb* wird nicht nur die Fiktion der Filmkulissen aufgebrochen, sondern auch die Fiktion der Vorstellung und des Denkens. Im Kopf eines Filmregisseurs wirbeln alle Realitäten und Fiktionen durcheinander. Er will sie bannen und fixieren in einem Drehbuch und einem Film. Gezeigt wird der Prozeß der Filmentstehung als autobiographische Krise. Jede Beobachtung, und jeder Einfall bringt eine Bilderkette aus Assoziationen und Erinnerungen hervor.

Hotel, Kurbad, Trinkhalle, Kurkonzert, Landschafts- und Stadtfragmente. Die gemeinsame Klammer ist der Film-Set. Zur Musik Wagners und Rossinis inszeniert Fellini in *Achteinhalb* ein Ballett aus Körpern, Gesichtern, Sätzen, Gedanken und Gesprächsfetzen. Hingetupfte Geschichten. Oberflächen. Jedes Gesicht und jedes Objekt wird Teil der neu entstehenden Fiktion. Jede Spaghetti-Nudel wird zum Faden der Ariadne. Aber das sich öffnende Wegesystem bleibt rätselhaft, torkelt von Bild zu Bild. Assoziationswalzer und Erinnerungstango. Erklärt das Vergangene das Jetzt, oder erklärt das Jetzt das Vergangene? Es gibt keine Antworten, die Fragen kippen aus dem Bild, mögliche Antworten werden jenseits des Films gesprochen. Die Erinnerungen quellen in sinnlichen Bildern hervor und verfangen sich in der Architektur der Räume. Die Realität ist nicht die Realität. Hinter der Oberfläche sind weitere Oberflächen. Zertrümmerungen und Neuzusammensetzungen. Häutungen. Bilder. Fellini zeigt den Prozeß der Filmentstehung als wahnwitzige Verschmelzung aus Autobiographischem, aus Erinnerung, Beobachtung, Beschreibung und fantastischer Übertreibung. Die Architektur bleibt eine mögliche Klammer, ein mögliches Gefäß, ohne das die Handlungssplitter für immer auseinanderfliegen würden.

Das Hinübergleiten aus der Welt in eine andere ist zum Thema geworden. Immer mehr Menschen wollen diesen Übergang sehen und lassen sich zu Tausenden durch die Studios in Hollywood, Berlin und Geiselgasteig fahren. Es ist für alle ein merkwürdiges Erlebnis, nicht mehr die Stadt selbst zu sehen, sondern nur noch leere Fassaden. Mit welcher Ernsthaftigkeit hier Realität nachgebildet wird, aber als leere Hülle ohne Funktion, irritiert. In den Filmstraßen beschleicht den Besucher die Angst, wie leicht Stadt ausgesaugt werden, zu einer starren Maske, einer Mumie, einem ausgestopften Wesen degenerieren kann. Man erkennt bestürzt, daß diese Außenhäute genügen, daß vielleicht die reale Stadt eine Lüge ist, eine Fiktion. Woran sich halten?

Heute hat sich zur Film-Fiktion noch die Fiktion des Fernsehens gesellt. Alle bisher gedrehten Filme werden dort immer wieder gezeigt. Erst mit dieser Möglichkeit haben sich die Filmräume den beherrschenden Platz in den Köpfen der Zuschauer gesichert, den sie vorher nicht hatten.

In den großen Studios der Welt werden heute mehr Fernsehfilme hergestellt als Kinofilme. Aber die Probleme sind im Grunde die gleichen geblieben.

Vielleicht besitzen die Serien heute im Alltagsleben genau den gleichen Stellenwert wie früher die Besuche von Marktplatz und Bridge-Club. Sie erweitern die alltäglichen Räume, erweitern den Freundes- und Bekanntenkreis. Jeder, der daran teilnimmt, hat auch ein Fenster hinaus in die *Lindenstraße* oder den *Marienhof*.

Wahrscheinlich stellen die *Tatort*-Filme den wichtigsten filmischen Beitrag der letzten zwanzig Jahre dar, den das Fernsehen in Deutschland produziert hat. In hundert Jahren wird sich in diesen Filmen unsere Zeit widerspiegeln wie die vierziger Jahre in der Schwarzen Serie Hollywoods. Zwar ist die Schwarzweiß-Stilisierung weggefallen, aber dafür sorgt eine differenzierte Beleuchtungstechnik für eine merkwürdige Künstlichkeit in den Räumen.

Der geschilderte Mordfall und seine mühsame Aufklärung ist immer in einer anderen Stadt angesiedelt und ereignet sich meist in den oberen Gesellschaftsschichten, eine Gelegenheit, modisch-coole Interieurs zu zeigen: In diesen überbelichteten und unbequemen Wohnungen, mit Blick auf einen Pool oder einen weitläufigen Garten werden Intrigen gesponnen, die die Konkurrenten schachmatt setzen sollen. Aber – wie immer – verstricken sich die Intriganten in ihrem eigenen Netz. Oft sind sie zwar nicht die Mörder – dazu bedarf es dann doch eines Täters, der noch bösartiger und skrupelloser ist –, aber sie alle wären dazu in der Lage gewesen, einen Mord zu begehen.

Um eine Gesellschaft zu schildern, reicht es nicht, sie von außen abzufilmen, man muß schon ihre Abgründe und Perversionen mit ins Bild bringen. Dazu ist ein Kriminalfall bestens geeignet. Es ist, als werfe man einen Stein ins Wasser und verfolge dann genau die Wellen und sein Absinken. Die Spannung als Strudel und Trichter, in den man hinabgezogen wird, ist wichtig für die Dramaturgie. Das wußten schon die alten Griechen und später die Hollywood-Regisseure.

Das Aufbauschema ist immer ähnlich: Man nimmt eine geradlinige Handlung, zerschneidet sie in fünfzig Einzelteile und setzt sie wie ein Puzzle zusammen, so, daß sich das geschlossene, verständliche Bild erst im letzten Moment ergibt (Aufklärung).

Diese Fragmentierung entspricht auch wieder in etwa der Schwarzen Serie: Es ist immer eine Frage der Wissens- und Informationsdosierung. Solange ich die Menschen kennenlerne, lerne ich auch ihre Taten kennen, dann entsteht ein Geflecht aus Vermutungen und Verdächti-

114. *Eight and a Half* (*Otto e Mezzo*); 1962; director: Federico Fellini, architecture: Piero Gherardi.

114. *Achteinhalb* (*Otto e Mezzo*), 1962; Regie: Federico Fellini, Architektur: Piero Gherardi.

gungen, jeder gegen jeden. Der ganze aufgestaute Haß kommt hoch, die Wut, aber auch die verdrängte Liebe. Ziel bleibt die Erkenntnis der Wahrheit, des wahren Sachverhalts. So gesehen sind Kriminalfilme – und *Tatorte* im besonderen – Aufklärungsfilme, Wahrheitssucherfilme. Der Kommissar als verdeckter Faust?

Die Tatsache, daß der Tod im Zentrum steht – der unnatürliche Tod, der Mord –, gibt diesen Filmen etwas Extremes. Sie gehen bis an die äußerste Grenze.

Neben den Ritualen der Aufklärung erfährt der Betrachter auch viel über die Räume dieser Gesellschaft: wie beispielsweise ein Polizeibüro aussieht, eine Gefängniszelle, ein Verhörraum, ein Gerichtssaal, die Wohnung des Kommissars, die Wohnung eines Models, die Wohnung eines erfolgreichen Kaufmanns usw. Da alles zusammen mit Kleidung, Sätzen, Meinungen und Gesichtern geliefert wird, ergibt sich das Bild einer Gesellschaft, heute, jetzt. Man kann diese Bilder mit der Realität vergleichen und seine Schlüsse ziehen.

In jedem Land der Welt gibt es ähnliche Serien und Phänomene.

115. Models in the Ufa Studios in Babelsberg for *Metropolis*, 1925/26; director: Fritz Lang, architecture: Otto Hunte, Erich Kettelhut and Karl Vollbrecht.
116. Shooting in the Ufa Studios in Babelsberg for *The Last Laugh*, 1924; director: Friedrich Wilhelm Murnau, architecture: Robert Herlth and Walter Röhrig.

115. Modellaufbauten in den Ufa-Studios in Babelsberg für *Metropolis*, 1925/26; Regie: Fritz Lang, Architektur: Otto Hunte, Erich Kettelhut und Karl Vollbrecht.
116. Dreharbeiten in den Ufa-Studios in Babelsberg für *Der letzte Mann*, 1924; Regie: Friedrich Wilhelm Murnau, Architektur: Robert Herlth und Walter Röhrig.

117, 118. Setting up a gigantic cyclorama of the film *I.N.R.I.* in the Berlin-Staaken film studios (1921). A contemporary studio report states: »Sermon on the Mount. Sandy hills rise in front of the cyclorama, with a picturesque encampment of about two thousand people. These are mobile hills that are simply pushed out after two to three hours, so that they can be turned back into wood and sand again outside. A wonderful view from the high scaffolding. The painted hills on the cyclorama blend with the architect's real work. Nature is outdone. Even the sun moves when Robert Wiene waves. It rises and sets as often as the director wants it to.«[10]

117, 118. Aufbau eines gigantischen Rundhorizonts für den Film *I.N.R.I.* in den Filmstudios Berlin-Staaken (1921). In einem zeitgenössischen Atelierbericht heißt es: »Bergpredigt. Vor dem Rundhorizont erheben sich Sandberge, malerisch belagert von rund zweitausend Menschen. Fahrbahre Berge, die man nach zwei oder drei Stunden einfach hinausschiebt, damit sie im Freien wieder zu Holz und Sand werden. Vom hohen Gerüst aus eine wundervolle Perspektive. Die gemalten Berge am Rundhorizont verschmelzen sich mit dem realen Werk des Architekten. Die Natur ist übertrumpft. Selbst die Sonne gehorcht dem Wink Robert Wienes. Sie geht auf und unter sooft der Regisseur es will.«[10]

119. Shooting in the Studios of Warner Brothers for *Rope,* 1948; director: Alfred Hitchcock, architecture: Perry Ferguson.
120. Shooting for *Münchhausen,* 1942; director: Josef von Baky, cartoon camera: Konstantin Irmen-Tschet.

119. Dreharbeiten in den Studios der Warner Brothers für *Cocktail für eine Leiche,* 1948; Regie: Alfred Hitchcock, Architektur: Perry Ferguson.
120. Dreharbeiten für *Münchhausen,* 1942; Regie: Josef von Baky. Trickkamera: Konstantin Irmen-Tschet.

121. Studio constructions in Geiselgasteig in Munich of the television series *Marienhof*: Architecture for television productions is similar to film architecture. A street and a little town square are built as realistic imitations, but the houses are just empty façades. Mock »town life« happens only during shooting.
122. Scene from *Lindenstraße,* 1985 (television series); director: Hans W. Geißendörfer.

121. Studioaufbauten in München-Geiselgasteig zu der Fernsehserie *Marienhof*: Die Architekturen für Fernsehproduktionen sind ähnlich wie für Filmaufnahmen. Ein Straßenzug mit kleinem Stadtplatz wird realistisch nachgebaut, aber die Häuser bestehen aus leeren Fassaden. Ein vorgetäuschtes »Stadtleben« findet nur während der Drehaufnahmen statt.
122. Szene aus *Lindenstraße*, 1985 (Fernsehserie); Regie: Hans W. Geißendörfer.

123, 124. Studio structures in Babelsberg for *The Ogre,* 1996; director: Volker Schlöndorff, architecture: Enzo Frigerio.

123, 124. Studioaufbauten in Babelsberg für *Der Unhold,* 1996; Regie: Volker Schlöndorff, Architektur: Enzo Frigerio.

World architecture

Hollywood is the secret world capital of dreams, subconscious and conscious fiction, and architecture. Hollywood is the Rome and the Versailles of the 20th and 21st centuries.[11] Here a new consciousness of space is created that embraces the world. These images, sets and film-spaces are fixed in every filmgoer's head. It may be that we saw the desert for the first time in the cinema, the Rocky Mountains, Greenland's glaciers or California's sandy beaches. We saw Western saloons and Al Capone's gloomy haunts. We saw Mexico's poverty-stricken huts and the Kennedys' penthouse apartments, the New Orleans jazz clubs and dream suites above the roofs of Manhattan. There was and is no corner of the globe into which the Hollywood film has not dreamed its way. Every cinemagoer in the world sees the same plot, the same images, the same faces, the same rooms, buildings, cities and streets. This medium's power to bind nations together can scarcely be overestimated. Film architecture is world architecture. All other architecture – our home town, street, house, flat – remains small in comparison, regional and affecting only a tiny area.

It is within the field of tension of these two aspects – small and regional, large and universal – that future architecture will develop. If film architecture is included, the language of the real architecture of buildings and streets could be enriched, and if the studio world is included real architecture could be jolted out of its banality.

Attempts are constantly made to break through the hermetics of individual areas. One has only to think of thirties and forties cinema architecture or Las Vegas's surreal advertisement architecture. The great neon advertisements that shine out in big cities all over the world share something of cinema reality's metaphysics. An interesting start has been made on built interplay in the Disney Worlds, in Epcot (Florida) and in the film street that has just been opened as the main entrance to Universal Studios in Hollywood. This is a pedestrian area flanked by shops, cafés, restaurants and cinemas. Every façade tries to cover up its essentially banal exterior with vivid additions and to translate it into urban meta-reality. This creates an excitingly surreal quality.

The charm of studio architecture lies in its fragmentary existence. The parts stand there as if cut out of reality. The city is not a complete whole, but just this corner, and behind it is the wood on the edge of the site. A sudden start and an abrupt end, no complete flow of reality. All structures in the open air have the charm of attempted surrealism. Unfortunately the studio buildings themselves are often trivial from the outside and look like factories. Despite this disadvantage the film studio cities of the world – Hollywood, London, Paris, Madrid, Rome, Munich, Berlin – could sometimes become the primeval cells of future urban regions and parks. It is possible to imagine that the fictitious buildings might some time burst out of these walls, make their way outside and form surreal islands, paths and squares in the meadows and copses. In between homes and offices are suspended in slender towers. Pieces of rock, waterfalls and glaciers float past. Dark cinema rooms are set in the glowing glaciers like black air-bubbles.

Weltarchitektur

Hollywood ist die geheime Welthauptstadt der Träume, der Fiktionen des Unterbewußtseins, des Bewußtseins und der Architektur. Hollywood ist das Rom und das Versailles des 20. und des 21. Jahrhunderts.[11] Hier wird ein neues weltumspannendes Raumbewußtsein geschaffen. Im Kopf eines jeden Zuschauers setzen sich diese Hintergründe, Bühnenbilder und Filmräume fest. Vielleicht hat man die Wüste zum ersten Mal im Kino gesehen, die Felsen der Rocky Mountains, die Gletscherberge Grönlands und die Sandstrände Kaliforniens. Man sah die Western-Saloons und die dunklen Räume Al Capones. Man sah die Hütten der armen Mexikaner und die Penthouse-Wohnungen der Kennedys. Man sah die Jazzclubs in New Orleans und die Traumsuiten über den Dächern von Manhattan. Es gab und gibt kaum einen Raumwinkel der Erde, in den sich der Hollywoodfilm nicht hineingeträumt hätte. Jeder Kinobesucher der Welt sieht die gleiche Handlung, die gleichen Bilder, die gleichen Gesichter, die gleichen Räume, Häuser, Städte und Straßen. Die völkerverbindende Kraft dieses Mediums ist kaum zu überschätzen. Filmarchitektur ist Weltarchitektur. Alle andere Architektur – die eigene Stadt, die eigene Straße, das eigene Haus, die Wohnung – bleibt dagegen klein, regional und in ihrer Wirkung nur auf ein winziges Umfeld beschränkt.

Im Spannungsfeld dieser beiden Aspekte – klein-regional und groß-weltumspannend – wird sich die künftige Architektur weiterentwickeln. Unter Miteinbeziehung der Film-Architekturen könnte die reale Architektur der Häuser und Städte in ihrer Sprache bereichert werden, und unter Miteinbeziehung der Studiowelt könnte die reale Architektur aus ihrer Banalität herausgekippt werden.

Es gibt immer wieder Versuche, die Hermetik der Einzelbereiche zu durchbrechen. Man denke nur an die Kinoarchitektur der dreißiger und vierziger Jahre oder an die surreale Reklamearchitektur von Las Vegas. Die großen Neonreklamen, die in allen Metropolen der Welt leuchten, haben etwas von der Metaphysik der Kinorealität. Interessante Ansätze für gebaute Wechselwirkungen gibt es in den Disney Worlds, in Epcot (Florida) und in der gerade eingeweihten Filmstraße, die zum Haupteingang der Universal-Studios in Hollywood führt. Hier handelt es sich um eine Fußgängerzone mit flankierenden Läden, Cafés, Restaurants und Kinos. Jede Hausfassade versucht, mit bildhaften Einbauten ihr an sich banales Äußeres zu umspielen und in eine städtische Metarealität zu übersetzen. Es entsteht ein spannender Surrealismus.

Der Reiz der Studio-Architekturen besteht in ihrem fragmentarischen Dasein. Wie herausgeschnitten aus der Realität stehen die Teile da. Stadt ist eben nicht ein großes Ganzes, sondern nur diese Ecke, dahinter beginnt der Wald des Außengeländes. Unmittelbares Beginnen und abruptes Aufhören, kein ganzer Realitätsfluß. Alle Aufbauten im Freien haben bereits den Reiz des angestrebten Surrealismus. Leider sind die Studiobauten selbst von außen oft trivial und sehen aus wie Fabriken. Trotz dieses Nachteils könnten die Filmstudio-Städte der Welt – Hollywood, London, Paris, Madrid, Rom, München, Berlin – einmal die Urzellen künftiger Stadtregionen und Parkanlagen werden. Man könnte sich vorstellen, daß die fiktiven Traumbauten diese Mauern einmal sprengen, daß sie nach außen wandern und in den Wiesen und Waldstücken surreale Inseln, Wege und Plätze bilden. Dazwischen hängen die Wohnungen und Büros in schlanken Türmen. Felsstücke, Wasserfälle und Gletscher treiben vorbei. In den leuchtenden Gletschern stecken die dunklen Räume der Kinos wie schwarze Luftblasen.

125. The first sight of Universal Studios in Hollywood is depressing: it looks just like a typical heavy industry plant. It is only when strolling around the halls that you find interesting situations. And further out on the site you find the sets you had been hoping for, like the square from *Back to the Future,* for example.

125. Der Blick auf die Universal–Studios in Hollywood ist zunächst deprimierend: Man glaubt eine der üblichen Großindustrie-Anlagen vor sich zu haben. Erst beim Herumwandern zwischen den Hallen entdeckt man interessante Situationen. Und weiter draußen im Gelände finden sich die Kulissenaufbauten, die man sich gewünscht hat, der Stadtplatz aus *Zurück in die Zukunft* beispielsweise.

126, 127. During a studio tour visitors are shown disasters more than anything else: burning factories, collapsing underground stations, attacks by sharks, etc. The break between reality and fiction remains visible only because the disasters can be controlled: the underground station that had been destroyed puts itself together again behind the visitor as though nothing had happened.

126, 127. Im Verlauf einer Studiotour werden dem Besucher vor allem Katastrophen vorgeführt: brennende Fabrikhallen, einstürzende U-Bahnstationen, Überfälle von weißen Haien usw. Der Riß zwischen Realität und Fiktion bleibt nur deswegen sichtbar, weil die Katastrophen beherrschbar sind: Hinter dem Besucher setzt sich die zerstörte U-Bahnstation wieder heil zusammen, als sei nichts geschehen.

128, 129. The reality of cities can be reproduced by sets. Only the outer skins radiate as images. They are crucial for effect and atmosphere. Erich von Stroheim's reconstruction of a hotel complex on the studio grounds in Hollywood.

128, 129. Die Realität der Städte ist durch Kulissen reproduzierbar. Nur die Außenhäute strahlen als Bilder ab. Sie sind entscheidend für die Wirkung und die Atmosphäre. Erich von Stroheims Rekonstruktion eines Hotelkomplexes auf dem Studiogelände in Hollywood.

Learning from Hollywood

Three places were described: the film itself with its architecture and rooms, the film studios with their fragmentary mock-ups of architectural realities and the actual cities with their buildings and homes. Human beings, hungry for experiences and images, wander between all three places, seeing and thinking. They absorb the fictions and realities as consciousness-images and are not concerned how deeply and valuably the individual image is rooted in reality. The main thing is that the image is there, visible and open to experience.

Actual urban architecture has scarcely absorbed these possibilities of deception, illusion. Contemporary architects like the concrete, geometrical order and the truth of the straight line. Most of them think even a large mirror is unserious and fraudulent. Even Baroque ceilings with their trompe-l'œil painting would be scorned today.

Here we need to pull down barriers and shift aesthetic and functional boundaries. Film images long ago conquered even the ugliest parts of cities, cellars, sewers, treatment plants and cooling towers, rainy junctions and lift-shafts. It would be interesting today to learn from cinema images and makeshift studio landscapes. It would be exciting to build just fragments, collages, empty outer skins, and to establish the needed functions here. Sometimes it would suffice to build a temporary structure, and not go for concrete, steel and glass.

Despite styles and fashions that keep reappearing – Post-Modernism, Deconstructivism etc. – our cities are boring, nerve-deadening in their banality. There is no elegance and no ruined areas, there are no Science Fiction upsurges and no areas of ghostly gloom. Cities have no language. They are silent and monotonous. They are dominated by tautologous one-dimensionality. No excitement, no entertainment, no art, no staging, no questioning, no traps, no dialogue, no superstructure. Even car and clothes design is more exciting than architecture.

In early times paintings by famous artists formulated aesthetic ideals. This is where they became images, always available to look at again, to question. Today painters' images have been joined by images from photography, advertising, the cinema, the new media and television. A veritable flood of images has flooded over earth's present inhabitants, and it is still flowing. Architecture is the slowest and most sluggish of all the arts. But it would be no problem today to stretch second and third skins in front of built structures; these would transform a city into a multi-dimensional reality. At night in particular it would be possible to work with projections, but also with changing façades and building shapes. Film architecture's immaterial quality and its fragmentary existence could influence cities. It is no longer enough to study architectural history, we must be familiar with film history as well, with its images, rooms and architecture.

Learning from Hollywood

Drei Orte wurden beschrieben: der Film selbst mit seinen Architekturen und Räumen, die Filmstudios mit ihren fragmentarischen Aufbauten von architektonischen Realitäten und die tatsächlichen Städte mit ihren Häusern und Wohnungen. Zwischen allen drei Orten vagabundiert der sehende und denkende, der erlebnis- und bildhungrige Mensch. Er nimmt die Fiktionen und Realitäten als Bewußtseinsbilder in sich auf, es ist ihm egal, wie tief und wertvoll das Einzelbild in der Wirklichkeit verwurzelt ist. Hauptsache, es ist da, sichtbar und dem Erlebnis offen.

Die tatsächliche Architektur der Städte hat die Möglichkeiten der Täuschung, der Illusion kaum in sich aufgenommen. Die heutigen Architekten lieben das Konkrete, die Ordnung der Geometrie und die Wahrheit der geraden Linie. Bereits ein großer Spiegel kommt den meisten unseriös und betrügerisch vor. Selbst barocke Deckenbilder mit ihren Illusionsmalereien wären heute verpönt.

Hier gilt es, Schranken abzubauen, ästhetische und funktionale Grenzen zu verschieben. Die Bilder des Films haben längst auch die häßlichsten Orte der Städte erobert, die Kellerräume, Kanalisationsrohre, die Kläranlagen und Kühltürme, die verregneten Kreuzungen und die Aufzugsschächte. Heute wäre es interessant, aus den Bildern des Kinos und aus den provisorischen Studio-Landschaften zu lernen, nur Fragmente zu errichten, Collagen, leere Außenhäute und hier die Funktionen einzurichten. Manchmal würde es auch genügen, temporär und provisorisch zu bauen, nicht gleich aus Beton, Stahl und Glas.

130. View from a hotel window in Santa Monica in the direction of Hollywood.

130. Blick aus einem Hotelfenster in Santa Monica in Richtung Hollywood.

Trotz immer wieder neu auftauchender Stile und Moden – Postmoderne, Dekonstruktivismus usw. – sind unsere Städte langweilig, von nervtötender Banalität. Es gibt weder Eleganz noch Ruinenzonen, es gibt weder science-fictionhafte Aufschwünge noch gespenstische Verdüsterungen. Die Städte haben keine Sprache. Sie sind stumm und monoton. Es herrscht tautologische Eindimensionalität. Keine Spannung, keine Unterhaltung, keine Kunst, keine Inszenierung, keine Infragestellung, keine Fallen, keine Dialoge, kein Überbau. Selbst das Design der Autos und der Kleider ist spannender als die Architektur.

In früheren Zeiten haben die Gemälde der berühmten Maler die ästhetischen Ideale formuliert, hier wurden sie zum Bild, immer wieder betrachtbar, immer wieder befragbar. Heute haben sich zu den Bildern der Maler die Bilder der Photographen, der Werbung, des Kinos, der neuen Medien und des Fernsehens gesellt. Eine wahre Bilderflut überspülte und überspült die heutigen Bewohner der Erde. Die Architektur ist die langsamste und trägste aller Künste. Dabei wäre es heute kein Problem, vor die gebauten Strukturen, zweite und dritte Häute zu spannen, die eine Stadt in eine mehrdimensionale Realität verwandeln würden. Man könnte – vor allem nachts – mit Projektionen arbeiten, aber auch mit wechselnden Fassaden und Hausformen. Die Immaterialität der Filmarchitekturen und ihre fragmentarische Existenz könnte Einfluß auf die Städte haben. Es genügt heute nicht mehr, Architekturgeschichte zu studieren, man muß auch die Filmgeschichte kennen, mit ihren Bildern, Räumen und Architekturen.

131, 132. Zugangsstraße zum Haupteingang der Universal Studios in Hollywood.

131, 132. Access road to the main entrance of the Universal Studios in Hollywood.

Notes

[1] Susan Sontag, *Über Fotografie*, Munich and Vienna, 1978, p. 105.
[2] Helmut Weihsmann, *Gebaute Illusionen*, Vienna, 1988, pp. 141 ff.
[3] Gottfried Knapp »Mythos Architektur« in: Gotthard Fuchs, Bernhard Moltmann, and Walter Prigge, *Mythos Metropole*, Frankfurt am Main, 1995, p. 98.
[4] Fred Gehler, Ulrich Kasten, *Fritz Lang. Die Stimme von Metropolis*, Berlin, 1990, p. 9.
[5] Dietrich Neumann in: *Kino – Movie,– Cinéma*, Berlin, 1995, p. 34.
[6] *Film ... Stadt ... Kino ... Berlin*, Berlin, 1987, p. 176.
[7] Hans Helmut Prinzler and Enno Patalas (eds.), *Lubitsch*, München and Luzern, 1984.
[8] Janine Pourray, *Die Entstehung von Waterworld*, Bergisch-Gladbach, 1995, p. 21 ff.
[9] Ebd., p. 158.
[10] *Film ... Stadt ... Kino ... Berlin*, a. a. O.
[11] Helmut Färber, *Baukunst und Film*, Passau, 1977, pp. 32 ff.

Anmerkungen

[1] Susan Sontag, *Über Fotografie*, München und Wien 1978, S. 105.
[2] Helmut Weihsmann, *Gebaute Illusionen*, Wien 1988, S. 141 ff.
[3] Gottfried Knapp, »Mythos Architektur« in: Gotthard Fuchs, Bernhard Moltmann und Walter Prigge, *Mythos Metropole*, Frankfurt am Main 1995, S. 98.
[4] Fred Gehler, Ulrich Kasten, *Fritz Lang. Die Stimme von Metropolis*, Berlin 1990, S. 9.
[5] Dietrich Neumann in: *Kino – Movie – Cinéma*, Berlin 1995, S. 34.
[6] *Film ... Stadt ... Kino ... Berlin*, Berlin 1987, S. 176.
[7] Hans Helmut Prinzler und Enno Patalas (Hrsg.), *Lubitsch*, München und Luzern 1984.
[8] Janine Pourray, *Die Entstehung von Waterworld*, Bergisch-Gladbach, 1995, S. 21 ff.
[9] Ibid., S. 158.
[10] *Film ... Stadt ... Kino ... Berlin*, op. cit.
[11] Helmut Färber, *Baukunst und Film*, Passau 1977, S. 32 ff.

Bibliography

Albrecht, Donald, *Design Dreams*, London, 1986.
Barsacq, Léon, *Le Décor du film*, Paris, 1985.
Bartetzko, Dieter, *Illusionen in Stein*, Hamburg, 1985.
Berg-Ganschow, Uta, and Wolfgang Jacobsen, *Film ... Stadt ... Kino ... Berlin*, Berlin, 1987.
Berger, Jürgen, *Production Design: Ken Adams*, Geiselgasteig, 1994.
Belach, Helga, and Wolfgang Jacobsen, *Buster Keaton,* Berlin, 1995.
Bergman, Ingmar, *Bilder*, Köln, 1991.
Bergman, Ingmar, *Mein Leben*, Hamburg, 1987.
Buñuel, Luis, *Mein letzter Seufzer*, Königstein im Taunus, 1983.
Chandler, Charlotte, *Ich Fellini*, Munich, 1994.
Färber, Helmut, *Baukunst und Film*, Passau, 1977.
Frewin, Leslie, *Dietrich. The Story of a Star*, New York, 1967.
Fuchs, Gotthard, Bernhard Moltmann, and Walter Prigge, *Mythos Metropole*, Frankfurt am Main, 1995.
Gehler, Fred, and Ulrich Kasten, *Fritz Lang. Die Stimme von Metropolis*, Berlin, 1990.
Giesen, Rolf, *Special Effects*, Ebersberg, 1985.
Gregor, Ulrich, and Enno Patalas, *Geschichte des Films*, Munich, Gütersloh and Vienna, 1973.
Harris, Robert A., and Michael S. Lasky, *The Films of Alfred Hitchcock*, Secausus, New York, 1976.
Heinzlmeier, Adolf, Jürgen Menningen, and Bernd Schulz, *Kino der Nacht*, Hamburg and Zurich, 1985.
Jacobsen, Wolfgang, *Babelsberg*, Berlin, 1992.
Jendricke, Bernhard, *Alfred Hitchcock*, Reinbek near Hamburg, 1993.
Karasek, Hellmuth, *Billy Wilder*, Munich, 1992.
Körte, Peter, *Humphrey Bogart*, Reinbek near Hamburg, 1992.
Mandelbaum, Howard, and Eric Myers, *Screen Deco*, New York, 1985.
Marner, Terence St. John, *Filmdesign*, London and New York, 1974.
Pourroy, Janine, *The Making of Waterworld*, New York, 1995.
Prinzler, Hans Helmut, *Chronik des deutschen Films*, Stuttgart and Weimar, 1995.
Renk, Herta-Elisabeth, *Ernst Lubitsch*, Reinbek near Hamburg, 1985.
Renoir, Jean, *Mein Leben und meine Filme*, Munich and Zurich, 1975.
Röder, Sabine, and Gerhard Storck, *Der dramatische Raum: Hans Poelzig*, Krefeld, 1986.
Sontag, Susan, *On Photography*, New York, 1977.
Sternberg, Josef von, *Fun in a Chinese Laundry*, New York, 1965.
Töteberg, Michael, *Fritz Lang*, Reinbek near Hamburg, 1985.
Valentine, Maggie, *The Show Starts on the Sidewalk*, Cambridge, Mass., 1994.
Weihsmann, Helmut, *Gebaute Illusionen*, Vienna, 1988.
Werner, Paul, *Film noir*, Frankfurt am Main, 1985.

Literatur

Albrecht, Donald, *Design Dreams*, London 1986.
Barsacq, Léon, *Le Décor du Film*, Paris 1985.
Bartetzko, Dieter, *Illusionen in Stein*, Reinbek bei Hamburg 1985.
Berg-Ganschow, Uta, und Wolfgang Jacobsen, *Film ... Stadt ... Kino ... Berlin,* Berlin 1987.
Berger, Jürgen, *Production Design: Ken Adams,* Geiselgasteig 1994.
Belach, Helga, und Wolfgang Jacobsen, *Buster Keaton*, Berlin 1995.
Bergman, Ingmar, *Bilder*, Köln 1991.
Bergman, Ingmar, *Mein Leben*, Hamburg 1987.
Buñuel, Luis, *Mein letzter Seufzer*, Königstein im Taunus, 1983.
Chandler, Charlotte, *Ich Fellini*, München 1994.
Färber, Helmut, *Baukunst und Film*, Passau 1977.
Frewin, Leslie, *Marlene Dietrich*, München 1984.
Fuchs, Gotthard, Bernhard Moltmann und Walter Prigge, *Mythos Metropole*, Frankfurt am Main 1995
Gehler, Fred, und Ulrich Kasten, *Fritz Lang. Die Stimme von Metropolis*, Berlin 1990.
Giesen, Rolf, *Special Effects*, Ebersberg 1985.
Gregor, Ulrich, und Enno Patalas, *Geschichte des Films,* München, Gütersloh und Wien 1973.
Harris, Robert A., und Michael S. Lasky, *The Films of Alfred Hitchcock*, Secausus, New York, 1976.
Heinzlmeier, Adolf, Jürgen Menningen und Bernd Schulz, *Kino der Nacht*, Hamburg und Zürich 1985.
Jacobsen, Wolfgang, *Babelsberg*, Berlin 1992.
Jendricke, Bernhard, *Alfred Hitchcock*, Reinbek bei Hamburg 1993.
Karasek, Hellmuth, *Billy Wilder*, München 1992.
Körte, Peter, *Humphrey Bogart*, Reinbek bei Hamburg 1992.
Mandelbaum, Howard, und Eric Myers, *Screen Deco*, New York 1985.
Marner, Terence St. John, *Filmdesign*, Hanau 1980.
Pourroy, Janine, *Die Entstehung von Waterworld*, Bergisch-Gladbach 1995.
Prinzler, Hans Helmut, *Chronik des deutschen Films*, Stuttgart und Weimar 1995.
Renk, Herta-Elisabeth, *Ernst Lubitsch*, Reinbek bei Hamburg 1985.
Renoir, Jean, *Mein Leben und meine Filme*, München und Zürich 1975.
Röder, Sabine, und Gerhard Storck, *Der dramatische Raum: Hans Poelzig*, Krefeld 1986.
Sontag, Susan, *Über Fotografie*, München und Wien 1978.
Sternberg, Josef von, *Das Blau des Engels*, München 1991.
Töteberg, Michael, *Fritz Lang*, Reinbek bei Hamburg 1985.
Valentine, Maggie, *The Show starts on the Sidewalk*, Cambridge, Mass., 1994.
Weihsmann, Helmut, *Gebaute Illusionen*, Wien 1988.
Werner, Paul, *Film noir*, Frankfurt am Main 1985.

Photo credits / Photonachweis

Archiv der Stiftung Deutsche Kinemathek Berlin 4–16, 17–18, 21, 23–28, 31–34, 36–44, 49–50, 53–54, 56–57, 59–61, 62–63, 65–67, 69–71, 73–75, 77, 79–80, 83, 85, 87–89, 94, 97, 98, 99, 110–113, 115–118
ARD-Filmredaktion (Stiftung Deutsche Kinemathek Berlin) 30, 68, 82, 93, 100
Atlas-Film (Stiftung Deutsche Kinemathek Berlin) 52
British Film Institute (Stiftung Deutsche Kinemathek Berlin) 84, 128–129
Columbia (Stiftung Deutsche Kinemathek Berlin) 114
Deutsche Universal-Film Berlin (Stiftung Deutsche Kinemathek Berlin) 96
EFPEKA, Film- und Presse-Korrespondenz E. Franke & W. Schneider (Stiftung Deutsche Kinemathek Berlin) 17
Filmverlag der Autoren (Stiftung Deutsche Kinemathek) 47, 48
Reinhard Görner 1–3
Heinz Köster (Stiftung Deutsche Kinemathek Berlin) 29
Loew's Inc. (Stiftung Deutsche Kinemathek Berlin) 51
Metro Goldwyn-Mayer (Stiftung Deutsche Kinemathek Berlin) 20, 90
The Museum of Modern Art (Stiftung Deutsche Kinemathek Berlin) 76
National Film Archive London (Stiftung Deutsche Kinemathek Berlin) 35, 45, 91, 102, 119
Paramount Pictures Corporation 72, 92, 101
Hans Dieter Schaal 121, 123–127, 130–132
Shanley Production Inc. (Stiftung Deutsche Kinemathek Berlin) 55
Tobis Filmkunst (Stiftung Deutsche Kinemathek Berlin) 46
Twentieth Century Fox (Stiftung Deutsche Kinemathek Berlin) 86, 95
Twentieth Century (Hans Dieter Schaal) 104, 105, 106, 107, 108, 109
UIP/FPF (Stiftung Deutsche Kinemathek Berlin) 64
United Artists Corporation (Stiftung Deutsche Kinemathek Berlin) 19
Warner-Columbia (Stiftung Deutsche Kinemathek Berlin) 22, 58, 78
WDF (Stiftung Deutsche Kinemathek Berlin) 122
WDR (Stiftung Deutsche Kinemathek Berlin) 81